RISE AN

RISE AND SIZZLE

Daily Communication and Presentation Strategies for Sales, Business, and Higher Ed Pros

BRIDGETT McGOWEN

FIRST EDITION, SECOND PRINTING

Library of Congress Control Number: 2019914851

ISBN: 978-0-9998901-2-7

Printed in the United States of America.

ACKNOWLEDGMENTS

AARON and PARKER

You mean so much to me, and I am nothing without you. You two are the reasons I rise, shine, sizzle, and grind each day. I love you … today, tomorrow, forever, and always.

SIMONE

You are absolutely the best friend I could ever have, and I have so much love for you. So much!

KIALA

You know how I feel about you. Done. End of story. Drop the mic. BMcHawk out.

CONTENTS BY DAY

CONTENTS BY TOPIC

audience-centric experience

audience-centric experience cont.

edtech presentations

effective communication

effective communication cont.

effective communication cont.

lecturing

personal branding cont.

presentation design

presentation skills

presentation skills cont.

presentation skills cont.

sales presentations

student-centric experience

student-centric experience cont.

INTRODUCTION

Do you know what makes people want to listen to you? What it takes to have a message that resonates? Others are inspired to stand up and take action when you understand your voice is perfect as it is, but that when you consciously use effective communication practices and articulate what matters, you will see success. You will have audiences laughing, reflecting, talking, learning, and leaning in wanting more from you.

I have combined nearly two decades of professional speaking experience; lessons learned from teaching at a community college, a four-year university, and an online university; years of traveling the country and designing and facilitating professional and faculty development; work in edtech sales; expertise in adult learning theory (andragogy); collaborations with sales and marketing leaders; and coaching clients on how to make presentations in a wide arena of industries to give you *Rise and Sizzle*.

So let's do this! Let's clear our throats, spend a month together, and get some real insight on effective communication and stellar presentations. Let's get ready to rise and sizzle!

-B

DAY 1
The Question 99% of Presentations Fail to Answer
effective communication | presentation skills

Have you ever sat in a meeting, a class, a teleconference, or in a webinar, reached the end, then thought, "Okay ... that's nice ... so ... what do I do now?"

Therefore, the question most presentations fail to answer is "What do I want the audience to know or to be able to do once this presentation has concluded?"

Each person's time is incredibly precious, and we all want as many minutes in the day as possible filled with meaningful endeavors. Okay. Well ... for the most part. Whether you want every last one of your 1,440 minutes of the day consumed with meaning or not, I'm sure you will agree that you want as few of those 1,440 minutes wasted as possible because let's face it; those meetings, calls, and webinars that conclude without you receiving a specific plan of attack (or any kind of plan of attack) can really rub you the wrong way!

As such, when you present—and this includes educators in the classroom, too—always give your audience a call-to-action (CTA). (And if you are in marketing, you are already familiar with this term, right?)

A CTA is instruction you give an audience that is meant to provoke an immediate (and meaningful) response from your listeners.

Marketers already understand the power behind a CTA; it's meant to move their target audiences from being passive to active, from being slightly interested to fully engaged. They want to convert leads or targets into confirmed customers who ultimately become happy, loyal, repeat customers, resulting in referrals! Happiness. Loyalty. Repetition. What's not to love?!

While it's important your audience has a memorable experience during your presentation and that it learns new

28

information or gains a new perspective on a concept, it is equally important to move the audience to actually use with what you presented—use it in a way that will inspire or change their lives, professions, or communities. You want them to use it in a way that will lead them to being happy, loyal, repeat customers who want to continue to engage with you.

Remember any time you present—and I firmly believe this includes a myriad of communication in which you engage such as phone conversations, social media posts, et cetera—consistently think to yourself "In what difference-making endeavor do I want my audience to join?" or "Now that everyone has heard this, what next steps do I need them to take?"

Based on what you present, think to yourself "What will extend their knowledge? What will extend their experience about this topic and create a richer meaning for them and those around them?"

Recommend they ...

- read a piece of material, then send a response to you or post a response to social media

- have a conversation with a colleague or send an email message to a colleague about X, then have the colleague do Y
- research Z, and add to the conversation by creating a post or other writing
- visit a specific place virtually or physically, and tell others what moved them and why others should visit, too

The simple rules to creating an effective CTA is it must directly connect to your session topic—easy, right—and it must move the audience to extend its thinking about the topic and to do so well after the conclusion of your presentation. That way, a metamorphosis of sorts occurs; your audience members go from inching along, listening during your talk to fluttering about, creating their own new knowledge. When you provide a CTA, your material is still on their minds, furthering your mission to transform your listeners into happy, loyal, repeat customers (or students)!

Educators, your CTA looks more like homework assignments and other types of assessments.

Oftentimes, it is suggested CTAs belong in only informative presentations and not in those meant to persuade or entertain, but I believe they belong in any speech or presentation where you want the audience to leave with useful information, feeling like their time was well spent.

DAY 1 SIZZLERS

1. How will calls-to-action show up in your life on a regular basis?

   _____

   _____

   _____

2. What calls-to-action do you need to give yourself right now? What do you need do you need to do differently each day?

   _____

   _____

   _____

3. In what ways will taking these specific actions impact you personally and/or professionally?

   _____

   _____

   _____

4. Why are they important to you? Others? Your success?

   _____

   _____

   _____

5. What are some actions you need to discontinue for the sake of your success?

_____

_____

_____

DAY 2
The Secret to Eliminate Information Overload
effective communication | presentation skills

As you effortlessly click from one screen to the next in your presentation or as you engage in conversations—especially on topics that are of particular interest to you—it is smooth as silk to you and makes all the sense in the world. In actuality, you may have made this presentation multiple times to various audiences in the past, so your script is in the back of your mind and at the ready. Whether it is your first or fifteenth time delivering the presentation or speaking on the topic, keep in mind, each audience is hearing it for the first time, and in either instance—the first iteration or the fifteenth—it becomes easy to throw in everything.

Take note that if you attempt to show and tell everything you know in your presentation, it becomes too much for the audience. Too much information can result in listeners getting confused or frustrated, asking questions you may not be able to answer or questions that require very involved responses that are further confusing, or listeners completely tuning out and/or engaging in other activities. In both the face-to-face and virtual presentation environments, you must provide manageable chunks of information and be careful of information overload, and here's how you do it.

Commit to solve only three problems.

Ask yourself "What are three big challenges the audience faces for which it is seeking solutions?" Then identify, from your material, that which will address those challenges or solve them altogether and present only that information.

In your opening statement to your audience, use those three challenges, needs, or interests to demonstrate for the audience what it will know or be able to do by the conclusion of the session. Use this actual phrase: "By the time we're done, you will know ... or be able to do ..." or "Let me tell you the three ways I have tackled that. First, ..." When you provide one of these kinds of statements, it accomplishes a number of things:

1. You clarify the takeaways.

2. It helps you remain focused.

3. It makes you feel empowered because you know the exact job you are there to perform.

4. It gives the audience a clear roadmap for what it can expect to receive while listening to you. It gives everyone a reason to listen to you.

DAY 2 SIZZLERS

1. In what other facets of your life will it prove beneficial to commit to solve only three problems and a commit to provide yourself with a roadmap?

   _____

   _____

   _____

2. What are three challenges that currently need your attention?

   _____

   _____

   _____

3. In what ways will addressing these challenges and creating a roadmap positively impact you personally and/or professionally?

   _____

   _____

   _____

4. Why is it necessary that you address these challenges in particular as opposed to other challenges?

   _____

   _____

   _____

5. Are there challenges you perceive as such but, upon closer inspection, really are not challenges at all but are opportunities? Explain.

_____

_____

_____

DAY 3
The #1 Rule for Presenting on Almost Any Service or Product

effective communication | presentation skills | sales presentations

Know the type of session you have been called upon to present. That's it. That's the number one rule for presenting on almost any service or product.

Not all presentations are the same. It's not just talk, but it's talking with a strategy.

Once you know the type of session you will present, then ...

... you lower your chances of having any missing or broken pieces, and you are fired-up, ready to approach the session with the right mindset and questions to keep your audience engaged and move you closer to your goals.

Will it be a demonstration, a training, or a professional or faculty development session? And one of the easiest ways to figure this out for sure is to ask the organizer "What do you want the audience to know or to be able to do upon the conclusion of this session?" Feel free to ask that of everyone connected to the session. Seriously. If you are working with five different people to set-up a presentation, then ask that question five times.

If it is a demo, then it is a pre-sale situation, and you have a point-and-click type of scenario. The audience has heard the name of the product and may have watched a video on it or had a brief conversation with you or another a sales representative about it, just scratching the surface. In a demo, you spend your time placing all of the features in the best light, methodically pointing out what the technology can do. In short, you are answering the questions "What is it?" and "What does it do?" There is not necessarily a lot of audience engagement during a demo because the audience is in discovery mode. Do take time for questions, but allow the audience to create its own questions such as "Can you go back to X?" or "What does Y do?"

If it is a training, then it is likely a post-sale situation. The customer has fallen in love with the product—or likes it a lot!—and has adopted it, and now you are showing the audience how to use the product. In this instance, you offer instruction and guidance for how to manipulate the product's options and features. Simply put, you are answering the questions "How do I use it?" and "What can I do with it?" In a training situation, there is not a lot of pressure on the presenter to build in opportunities for engagement because engagement tends to be organic. Trainings are meant for the audience to have a hands-on experience. You are not completely off the hook, though, when it comes to audience engagement) because you'll want to have questions that address comprehension. Show the steps again, then ask, "What questions do you have about ____?" and fill in the blank with the task/functionality you just showed. (And I hasten to add avoid asking "Is everyone clear? and here's why: There will be someone who is *not* clear but who will not self-identify because the tenor of the question suggests everyone *should* be clear. Additionally, because this is a training, the kinds of questions you ask will be different from those you ask in a professional development setting because in this instance, you want to check for understanding.)

Finally, if the session is professional or faculty development, then it is post-sale and goes beyond a training. In a professional development scenario, you combine the what and the how to advance and expand the audience's understanding of the product, and you move into explaining the why and showing the power of the product. In a professional or faculty development environment, you are answering questions such as "Why should I use it?" and "Why is it a benefit?" In a professional or faculty development instance, you want to give participants time to think about what the information means for them and those in their circles; to explore the possibilities; to become cognitively moved, to grow a deeper connection to your brand, and to become more energized than ever before to engage with the product.

DAY 3 SIZZLERS

1. What is a process already in place in your personal or familial life that you should simplify for yourself (or others)?

   _____

   _____

   _____

2. What is a process already in place in your professional life that you should simply for yourself?

   _____

   _____

   _____

3. What will result from this simplification?

   _____

   _____

   _____

4. Why should you bother? How will the simplification benefit you?

   _____

   _____

   _____

5. What are the precise steps you will take to create this simpler existence?

DAY 4
Five Questions You Must Answer in an Edtech Sales Presentation
edtech presentations | effective communication |
presentation skills | sales presentations

Presenting edtech to what may seem like a low-tech audience can sound like high stress, but it does not have to be.

Use the following five questions as the foundation of a five-part organization to your presentation. Answer them, and your audience will go from no tech to edtech in no time.

(And as a bonus, tech-savvy audiences benefit from having these questions answered, too!)

How will using this technology ...

1. make faculty members' lives easier without causing any complication for them or their students when it's time to start using it? It's the elephant in the room as one higher education consultant once told me. Educators already have full plates. If it's not one report that's due, then there's a scheduling conflict that needs fixing. If it's not one committee meeting to attend, then it's another one for which an agenda needs to be prepared. Spending an inordinate (or any significant) amount of time trying to learn a new technology is usually not at the top of their "Boy, I Cannot Wait to Do This!" lists. If you have an outstanding and accommodating training program and stellar tech support that will get and keep faculty and students up and running, detail that with much specificity.

2. create a more engaging in-class teaching experience for faculty members? If a tech tool has the functionality to make a faculty member even more dynamic and enthusiastic in the classroom, bring concepts to life, or allow for real-time formative assessments, for example, then you're talking their language. Show that tool. Show that functionality. Show them what technology can do to make class sessions more enjoyable and more productive. Technology is not a tool that will replace the educator; it is a tool—that's it—a tool that enhances what they already do.

3. create a more engaging in-class learning experience for students? Will your technology make it easier for faculty to conduct classroom assessment techniques, low-stakes and informal activities that gauge learning and understanding? Can using your technology create an effortless ability among faculty to reference the textbook and highlight important points for students? Will it have students asking questions, volunteering ideas, collaborating with classmates? Can your technology move students to read *gasp* BEFORE they arrive to class?! Demonstrate how any—or better yet—ALL of that can happen with your digital solution.

4. improve out-of-class conversations between faculty and students? Extending course conversations beyond the classroom's four walls is every educator's dream. What mathematics professor wouldn't *love* to walk up on his/her students as they sit in the student union discussing the acute and obtuse angles observed on their slices of pizza? Okay. A long shot. But if a technology offers a discussion board that can keep the momentum going after the class session has ended, one perhaps where you can invite guest speakers from across town or across the globe to engage in a conversation with your students, then you can get educators' attention.

5. help students spend time outside of class preparing for the next class session? There's homework, then there's homework. The type that moves students to think critically and motivates them to engage in the course material *before* arriving to class is just the type educators want. A technology that gives students opportunities to experience bursts of learning in the fashion to which they have become accustomed to receiving information is just the ticket. Show educators how your digital tool moves psychology students from barely knowing about William Perry's Theory of Moral and Cognitive Development to them showing up in class, ready to completely rewrite the theory!

DAY 4 SIZZLERS

1. What can do today that will make someone else's life easier?

   _____

   _____

   _____

2. How satisfied are you with how frequently you engage with others and how frequently you make new connections? What should you do differently?

   _____

   _____

   _____

3. Will you commit to making at least one new connection each week? What will be your strategy for doing so?

   _____

   _____

   _____

4. Why should you bother? Why should you endeavor to make new connections?

   _____

   _____

   _____

5. What are at least two connections you need to make that you have been putting off? How will making these connections prove beneficial to you?

_____

_____

_____

DAY 5
THE Ultimate Elevator Pitch
audience-centric experience | effective communication | networking | personal branding

It's the line you dread hearing, especially if you are just starting out in your industry or if you are new to entrepreneurship ...

"So ... what do you do?"

It's not that you do not love what you do or that you do not want to proclaim your professional passion. It's the fact you have not properly prepared an answer to this question, so you defer to giving your title. WRONG! (It happens all the time. I'll ask someone "What do you do?" and I get his/her title, which prompts me to follow-up with "Okay. So what do you do?")

The key relevance of an elevator pitch is you narrow down to a succinct 30-second presentation the what, why, and how of your profession; you want to inform your listener in a focused way that makes the listener want to say "Really?! That's what you do?!" and that makes the listener start thinking of either ways to do business with you or the connections he/she can make for you. In short, the elevator pitch must clarify what you do that helps others be better at what they do.

You must clarify what you do that helps your listener be better at what he/she does.

Use this four-part approach every time you pitch yourself or your business, and you make it very clear to your listener what you do, the results you bring your clients, how you're different from your competitors, and how you're on your way (or already there!) to the top floor!

1. Your name, *your title that everyone will understand/what it is you do, and your company affiliation.

2. One sentence identifying your target client, target client's desired result, and unwanted or inconvenient steps you help the client avoid so he/she can achieve that desired result.

3. **Your name and your company affiliation

4. Tagline

Let's check out how this looks:

1. NAME, TITLE, AND COMPANY: My name is Bridgett McGowen, and I am a professional speaker at BMcTALKS.

2. TARGET CLIENT, DESIRED RESULT(S), AND INCONVENIENT STEP(S): I help professional women who want to speak with power and executive presence but who do not want to waste time reading books and watching videos that cannot give them real and honest feedback on their presentation skills. (This sentence is said in chunks so the audience really hears it.)

3. NAME AND COMPANY: Bridgett McGowen of BMcTALKS.

4. TAGLINE: Be seen. Be heard. Be great!
Now let's put it all together.

My name is Bridgett McGowen, and I am a professional speaker at BMcTALKS. I help professional women who want to speak with power and executive presence but who do not want to waste time watching videos that cannot give them real and honest feedback on their presentation skills. Bridgett McGowen of BMcTALKS. Be seen. Be heard. Be great!

Naturally, if you are having a one-on-one conversation, you would likely leave out numbers 3 and 4.

A quick note: Avoid using contractions; say all words in their entirety. One contraction in particular that causes problems is "can't" because if one is not listening closely or is not paying close attention, then it can be mistaken for "can."

Clarify your target client, at least one desired result that you provide, and unwanted or inconvenient steps that your target customer can avoid while still achieving the desired result because of how awesome you are!

*Avoid giving your official title because rarely does a title have meaning for your listeners unless it's one of those straightforward titles such as "hair stylist" or "realtor." If you want to set yourself apart from others who have the same straightforward titles, then get away from relying too heavily on your title in your elevator pitch, and focus more on number 2 above. Additionally, while C-suite and vice president titles are impressive, avoid using those tittles, too, because when you do, all it communicates is "I have an important title." Furthermore, titles that are less straightforward such as "Director of Professional Development and Strategic Alliances" can be too much to unravel to arrive at, in laymen's terms, what a person does. Always endeavor to first communicate to others what you do and the difference you make in the lives of others.

**If your company name and your tagline are similar to each other, and it almost sounds like you are repeating yourself, then when you get to numbers 3 and 4, then consider saying the company name, then your name, then the tagline.

DAY 5 SIZZLERS

1. Why is it so important to move away from identifying with a job title and to move closer to identifying with the difference you make?

2. What is your "it" factor? What is your secret sauce that makes you different from others who also do what you do?

3. How will knowing your "it" factor impact your confidence and how others perceive you?

4. Why is it necessary for you to consistently communicate your "it" factor?

5. Why is it critical that others know your "it" factor?

_____

_____

_____

DAY 6
Do This, and No One Will Ever Miss Your Class (or Presentation) Again!

audience-centric experience | effective communication | lecturing | presentation skills | student-centric experience

You heard the lectures from your parents growing up. Then you went to school and heard even more lectures. Once you arrived to college, you were just about lectured-out. But now you teach (or you make presentations as part of the work you do), and you do what you know best. You lecture! Okay. Perhaps you do not, but I know when I first stepped into the college classroom to teach in 2002, that's exactly what I did!

Regardless of whether lecturing is the focal point of your teaching (or presentation) or not, remember the points herein to help you work toward achieving your goals while inviting student participation during the session. If you do so—if you try these strategies—then your students will walk away tuned in and having actually learned, and you will leave class with a sense of having achieved new heights in student engagement! (And you'll notice "presentations" keeps sneaking in; these strategies are applicable to anyone who stands before an audience and who wants to make it a captive one, leaving everyone wanting more. Therefore, if you present in any capacity, replace "lecture" or "class" with "presentation," and charge on!)

People are fully engaged for only the first 18 to 30 seconds someone is speaking to them before "out" thoughts start creeping in—thoughts such as dinner plans, errands to run, email messages that need responses, et cetera, et cetera. (And be honest; you are having "out" thoughts right this very moment! Come back to me!) At the start of your lecture, think of how you can help students become more metacognitive about their thinking and more engaged in what you provide them during your session.

Within the first five minutes of class, you must pump up, pull in, pass the microphone, and provide information to your students. Pump up or excite your students by making connections between the session topic and them, and pull then in and pass the microphone by making the session all about what they will get out of it and by getting input from them. The inform part is easy; it is the objective material you provide in your lectures. It is the pump up and pull in parts that require a little more effort. Get students excited simply by telling them how their lives, success, abilities will be exponentially enhanced with what you presented in that class, that if they can learn X, Y, and Z, then all of the A, B, and C that can come their way.

Think back to the start of this reading and how I indicated that if you do ____, then ____ would happen. You were excited! You wanted (and did!) immediately dive into reading, right?

This is good, but you may ask "Bridgett, how do I keep the momentum going beyond the first five minutes of class?" This is how:

Your course content is like a buffet; you have so much information you can provide students. At the same time, your students' minds are similar to buffet plates. In 1956, George A. Miller formulated the chunk concept as he presented evidence that the working memory is limited in capacity. Miller stated that working memory could hold seven (plus or minus two) chunks of information at once, but it is now thought that the number is closer to four or five bits of information.

The takeaway is if a learner's working memory is full, then the excess information will just drop out.

If you are explaining a complex concept that requires the learner to hold several factors in mind to understand it, then there is a good chance the learner is not retaining much of what you say.

You need to chunk information into bite-sized pieces and present it in organized sections.

So the final point is to ensure you provide students with chunks of information—no more than twelve to fifteen minutes of content—then pause and let them digest that information. Use a formative assessment so they can process the information and understand what it really means, then give them another chunk of information.

You may have heard the lessons a hundred times and can regurgitate the material at the drop of a dime; students are hearing your content for the first time. They need time to think. Consider this: If I ask you a question as simple as "What did you have for dinner yesterday," you would have to stop and think. The questions you ask students are far more involved. As such, give your students that necessary time to process much more complex content.

You may find twelve minutes is too long; know it is not a hard and fast rule. You know your students best; if you see they are starting to check out, pause to provide a classroom assessment technique, and give them time to fully comprehend what you have delivered. This eliminates overwhelm and positively impacts learning every single time.

DAY 6 SIZZLERS

1. Consider the points covered in Do This, and No One Will Ever Miss Your Class (or Presentation) Again! How can you apply them when you engage in one-on-one conversations?

   _____

   _____

   _____

2. How will your conversations be improved as a result of putting in place the techniques?

   _____

   _____

3. Will making connections or providing bite-sized pieces of information be the most helpful to your listeners?

   _____

   _____

   _____

4. How aware are you of the body language of your listeners? Do you need to improve your awareness? Why or why not?

   _____

   _____

_____

5. What can you do or say to ensure your listeners are always engaged?

_____

_____

_____

DAY 7
Start on Time. End on Time.
audience-centric experience | effective
communication | presentation skills

No thrills. No frills. Begin a presentation on time, and complete it on time as it shows respect for the audience's time. When you fail to do either or both, then the message you send to your audience is "Your time is not important to me." Plain and simple.

Your audience members who have shown respect by arriving early or on time are due the same respect. You may ask what to do when you have a glitch with the technology that causes a delay or what to do if a person in a key position has yet to arrive and you must wait for his/her arrival before you begin. Don't you worry for a second. You've got this.

If that or any other instance is the case, then let the audience know at the official start time and proceed to engage everyone in a meaningful exercise. A quick statement to this effect works: "Thank you for coming today. We are fixing a technical glitch/we do not want to begin without your division chairperson. We will get started shortly. In the meantime, please write down what you want to get out of today's session, then discuss it with the colleague sitting next to you." Or choose to use this time to answer questions audience members have. Make valuable use of everyone's time.

Additionally, ensure you avoid using phrases such as "If I had more time, I would ..." or "For those of you who can remain a few minutes after the presentation, I'll tell you ...." It suggests the organizer failed to schedule ample time for your message. However, you are in control of your message. As such, it is your responsibility to ensure you request the appropriate amount of time you need or that you tailor your presentation to fit in the amount of time that has been allotted for you.

Additionally, it is unfair to penalize those—positioning them to miss out on additional details—for operating in accordance with the advertised start and end times of the presentation.

Audience participation can become so robust until you may find yourself having to jettison some material. Know before your presentation and during your practice time what information can be left out so you are prepared if you find yourself in a position where you need to omit material in the interest of ending on time. That information should be content that would not interfere with the audience being able to understand your message and/or act as a result of having heard your presentation. If you have to omit any information, simply omit it without any mention to the audience, and keep it moving. You are the only one who will know you did not cover it. And the bonus is ... you might have a piece of material that positions you to schedule a follow-up performance!

Finally, the audience tends to mentally (and sometimes physically) check-out when you approach the final minutes of your presentation. Do you remember when you were in a face-to-face class? You watched the clock, and the closer it got to the last minutes of the class, the less engaged you were with what the teacher said. The same goes for any other audience. Ensure you plan to always include a call to action for your audience. Now that they have heard your presentation, what do they do now? Factor in ample time to answer that question for both you and your listeners.

The takeaway? Start on time; end on time.

DAY 7 SIZZLERS

1. In what other areas of your life should you put more focus and attention on time, amounts of time dedicated to endeavors, and/or timeliness?

    _____

    _____

    _____

2. How will this impact you and others for the better?

    _____

    _____

    _____

3. What can cause you to lose track of time or fail to be on-time?

    _____

    _____

    _____

4. What can you do differently to be more mindful of your time and the time of others?

    _____

    _____

    _____

5. Are there activities that do not need as much (or any of your time)? In what can you improve how you spend your time?

_____

_____

_____

DAY 8
Why Should Anyone Bother to Listen to You?
audience-centric experience | effective communication | presentation skills

That's a pretty harsh question, isn't it? Why should anyone bother to listen to you?

But it's that very question that gets those expert speakers to the point where they are delivering killer presentations.

It's not magic.

It's not a fluke.

It's not that they have something in their DNA.

What they do is they give the audience what it wants. They think to themselves "If I was in the audience, then what would I want to hear? What do I need to hear? What will make me sit up and pay attention? What does the presenter need to say or do that will make me feel like this was time well spent and not just an opportunity to fill some minutes in the day?" Then they set out to give just that. And by giving the audience what it wants to hear, you answer the question of "Why should the audience care?" And that's the game-changer.

If you do not give adults a reason to listen ... if you do not set out to immediately get the arms uncrossed ... to quickly move the minds from thinking about everything but your presentation ... to expeditiously put the attitudes in the right place ... then you run the risk of the audience tuning you out before you even get started.

And I know you know what I'm talking about. You've done it yourself. You may have even done it as recently as this week! You walk into a meeting, and you're thinking "This had better be good and not something that could have been sent in an email message because I have a million things to do and not enough time in the day to get them done."

Time is an audience's most precious commodity. Period. End of story. Wrap it up, and stick a bow on it. An adult's time has to be carefully treated because it feels like we have less and less of it with each passing day.

Now, you can look at approaching your presentations in a number of ways, but here are two specific points of view I need you to consider:

1. either you give the presentation you would love to hear if you were seated in the audience

OR

2. you give the presentation that you *think* the audience wants to hear.

Now, I know the two may be one in the same; they *can* be one in the same if you make the first point of view your priority ... if you simply ask yourself "If I was in the audience, then what would I want to hear? What do I need to hear? What will make me sit up and pay attention? What does the presenter need to say or do that will make me feel like this was time well spent and not just a way to fill time?"

Make it clear why everyone should listen. They should listen because this information is going to ...

change lives ...

create happiness ...

improve marketability ...

reduce stress ...

increase sales ...

boost motivation ...

enhance health ...

promote productivity ...

You get the idea.

Tell them what they will know or be able to do, then school them. Do not ever let people leave your presence without feeling like you did not uplift them, help them, or develop them in some way. When you become known as someone who is going to deliver thoughtful, helpful, important, and needed information, then people cannot wait for your next presentation. They cannot wait for the next time to engage with you. Can. Not. Wait.

DAY 8 SIZZLERS

1. If you are in an audience, what makes you pay attention to a speaker?

   _____

   _____

   _____

2. What should you say that will grab and keep your listeners' attention?

   _____

   _____

   _____

3. Why should the audience care about your message?

   _____

   _____

   _____

4. What can you say to uplift audiences?

   _____

   _____

   _____

5. What changes do you need to make to your messages to ensure they are consistently thoughtful, helpful, important, and necessary?

DAY 9
Here's How You Get Others to Fall in Love with Your Product

audience-centric experience | effective communication | presentation skills | sales presentations

Have you ever been in the middle of a sales presentation where you demonstrated a product's feature, then you asked, "Isn't this great?" or "Wouldn't this be useful to you?!" and you got crickets?

Here's why this happens:

People buy what will benefit them and what will help them with the work they do, not the features a sales professional finds down-right fabulous. Until your prospective customers see for themselves the fabulousness you see, until they personally connect to the product, they will still think "I'm not sold because I don't see what's in it for me." But there is a small tweak you can make to your questioning techniques that fosters this oh-so-important personal connection.

You likely know by now the first pointer is as follows: avoid pointing out what the audience should find interesting.

But allow me to pause for a moment.

Avoid doing away with having those pointers at hand; keep those ideas in your back pocket in the event you need to draw the audience's attention to them, but first and foremost, ask the audience members what they find beneficial, helpful, useful, et cetera. Here are some examples of how you might do that:

Instead of "Don't you like X?!" ask, "What do you like the most about X? "

Instead of "Isn't Y interesting?!" ask, "What do you find most interesting about Y?"

Instead of "You would use this, right?" ask, "How do you see yourself using this?"

And a word of caution with asking questions: Make sure you give the audience time to process. After you ask the audience a question but before you call on volunteers to respond to the question, count to seven in your head to give everyone time to think about the question, think of an answer, and then verbalize it. (I learned this great tip from a former colleague many many moons ago when she volunteered to observe one of my class sessions.)

What makes this approach—the audience identifying a benefit—so impactful is if you have a room of 10 people, instead of zooming in on the one or two amazing features *you* want to highlight, you end up with 10 amazing features the *audience* wants to highlight that are personal, useful, and beneficial to those 10 participants.

And just like that *finger snap* you have gotten them to see your product as a gift— to see for themselves what's beneficial to them and to make a personal connection with the product.

DAY 9 SIZZLERS

1. How effective is your questioning strategy in general? Are you consistently able to get the information you need?

   _____

   _____

   _____

2. How well do people respond to your questions? Are they confused, or do they dive right in with responses?

   _____

   _____

   _____

3. How often do you ask follow-up questions, especially as a means for building rapport and interest?

   _____

   _____

   _____

4. What will you do differently with the way you ask questions, going forward, to better capture the imaginations of others?

   _____

   _____

   _____

5. What will be the benefit, going forward, to paying more attention to and/or adjusting your questioning strategies?

_____

_____

_____

DAY 10
Friends Don't Let Friends Design Ugly Slide Decks
presentation design | presentation skills

For some, PowerPoint (PPT) presentations are becoming a tool of the past, but for those who still use them—*hand in the air* that would be me!—or PPT's Apple cousin, Keynote, read on! (Not so fast! So you do not use PPT or Keynote. That's cool. I know you have a colleague who uses one or the other, and you have been looking to offer some constructive criticism, right? I knew it! Let's charge ahead!)

Voyage with me into the mind of an English instructor. Come on. I promise it will all make sense in a minute.

Upon first glance at a student's paper, an instructor, especially an English instructor, can immediately ascertain if the paper is "A" work or otherwise. The spacing is nicely done; margins are the right size; the font is our all-time favorite, Times New Roman, at a 12-point size; headings are in place; you even see a few citations that are properly formatted. You can feel it; this is a winner, and you want to read on! Right?! (Or am I alone on this one?)

Just as educators may be a touch leery of the contents or the quality of the contents of a paper if it is poorly formatted, just as we may be skeptical of a restaurant that looks a little shady (although I've been known to visit my fair share of greasy spoons), or just as a website with a questionable design (*biting lip) gives us pause, your presentations can find themselves under similar scrutiny by your audiences. A couple of small presentation design details you may not have considered are ...

Should you use a dark background or a light background? How do you know when you should use one or the other, and why does it even matter? And what size font should you use?

Here are the answers.

If you are presenting to an audience of 50 or more, then your presentation template should have a dark background with light color text.

If you are presenting to an audience with fewer than 50 in the audience, then use a light background with dark text.

In both instances, this makes it easier on audience members' eyes.

And here's how you know if your text is larger enough: print a slide and place it on the floor. If you can read the text with no problem from a standing position, then the font is large enough for your presentation. A good rule of thumb is your font should be no smaller than 28-point, titles should be at least 32-point, and you should have no more than about five bullets of information per slide with about five to seven words per bullet.

However, my personal preference has led me to a more minimalistic approach where I provide a high-quality, high-impact graphic with only a few words or one or two bullets of information on a slide because graphics stir emotions unlike any bulleted words can ever stir them. My go-to's for snagging graphics are www.pexels.com, www.pixabay.com, and www.unsplash.com

When searching for images on a stock photography site (e.g., an image of a boat), try different synonyms of the word (e.g., ship), specific types/categories of the word (e.g., yacht, steamboat, canoe, etc.), or related words (e.g., fishing, sailing, cruise, et cetera). Consider using a thesaurus or keyword lists on actual image pages to identify other keywords you can use in your image search.

Remember *you* want to be what draws in your audience, not your presentation software. Always position yourself so you, your words, and your energy are more important than anything you could ever flash up on a screen!

DAY 10 SIZZLERS

1. How well do you work to draw people unto you? Are there changes you should make?

   _____

   _____

   _____

2. What areas of your life—personally or professionally—wll benefit from a redesign?

   _____

   _____

   _____

3. What needs minimizing in your life? (e.g., working too much) What do you need to increase? (e.g., time with family or friends)

   _____

   _____

   _____

4. What rules of thumb can you add to your life? Are there rules you can create for work engagements? Personal commitments?

   _____

   _____

   _____

5. How will these rules positively impact you?

_____

_____

_____

DAY 11
8 Ways to Make Meetings More Meaningful
effective communication | effective meetings | presentation skills

Every one of your meetings can arouse interest, energy, and excitement from your team. No one will fall asleep in them. Your teams will stop looking at their watches, the clocks at the back of the room, and the time on their devices. They will be more open to what you and others have to offer. Your meetings can become some of the brightest, most productive parts of the week.

So how is it done?

Here's the *Readers Digest* version:

1. Be happy to be there!
2. Provide the meeting goal(s).
3. Clarify how you will handle questions.
4. Remember time is a person's most precious commodity.
5. Hear from others.
6. Hear from others more!
7. Thank someone.
8. Assign action items.

1. Be happy to be there! Have you ever attended a meeting and immediately knew the leader did not want to be there? Even before she opened her mouth, you could tell by her body language that she was would rather be anywhere but there. And then when he opened his mouth, you knew unequivocally this was not going to be the best part of your day. Meeting-goers take their leads from the person at the front of the room. His temperament will dictate others' temperament; her attitude will drive the attitudes of others. If you show you are happy to be there, then others feel it, and you see positive returns.

Even if you have not-so-happy news to deliver, you still want to demonstrate you are pleased, honored, and happy to be the one with the opportunity to lead your team through challenges and triumphs.

2. Provide the meeting goal(s). Do this within the first few minutes of your meeting along with the agenda, and use power words now and throughout the meeting. Break away from meeting for the sake of a meeting or because it is a requirement handed down by the powers that be. Even if that is indeed the case, you can make it more meaningful; you must because your team is depending upon you and its leader to do so.

Make a simple statement such as "Upon the end of this meeting, you will ...

... know X, Y, and Z."
... be ready for A, B, and C."
... understand what's next in ___ and what you need to do and by when to get ready."

You get the idea. It's akin to a teacher stating the objectives of a course in the syllabus. Students want to know what new knowledge they will have and what new actions they will be able to perform after spending a term in that course. The same goes for team members who want to know the exact same in your meetings. When you do that—clarify the meeting goal(s) right away—then you have a more engaged, attentive team because you have given a roadmap for how time will be spent. (When possible, send the meeting agenda to attendees beforehand; that helps mentally prepare everyone prior to arriving to the meeting. They need to have an idea of how their time will be spent.)

3. Clarify how you will handle questions. Will you take them throughout the meeting (not advisable), or will you reserve time at the end to take them? It is recommended questions are held until the end so as to not get in the way of your momentum, interrupt the flow of the meeting, or end up having someone (or you!) going down a rabbit hole. Additionally, there is always the possibility a question will be asked prematurely, eating into valuable meeting time. A premature question is one where its answer will be covered later in the agenda. However, if you are particularly skilled at leading meetings, then you are at liberty to take questions throughout. Either way, let the audience know when the floor will be open for questions, and ensure you put a time limit the Q&A segment by saying, "We will take five minutes for questions," for example, then take no more than those five minutes.

4.   Remember time is a person's most precious commodity. As such, start on time, and end on time. Leaders are considered thoughtful and respectful when they are careful to watch the clock and adhere to appointed end times. And as a result, teams tend to be thoughtful toward and respectful of leaders who respect their time. Team members who arrive on time should not be punished and have to wait for latecomers.

Furthermore, team members may have other commitments and obligations they scheduled based on the stated meeting end time; avoid placing them in uncomfortable positions of having to choose between remaining in your meeting that has run late and being disrespectful of the other commitment or feeling disloyal and excusing themselves from your meeting that has gone over time.

5.   Hear from others. Provide meeting attendees with chunks of information—no more than three to five minutes of content—then pause and let them digest/discuss that information. (The three to five minutes is not set in stone; you can tell when your team is starting to get the glazed donut look. When you see that, it's time to switch things up!) Make room for others' comments and input; bring other voices into the meeting so you are all singing the same chorus as opposed to everyone listening to one person's solo. When others feel they have contributed to a discussion, solution, challenge, or idea, they are inspired and are more likely to embrace and move forward.

6. Hear from others more! Work should not always be about work, right? Find out a curious or interesting fact about your team members, and allow for time for them to find out learn about each other. I recall taking about five minutes in a meeting to have a team write down on index cards something they had done that was unique, interesting, or that which they believed no one else in the room had done. I collected them, read them aloud, and if someone had done that same thing, then they were to high-five each other. Can you believe the fun we had learning one of our teammates once wore a mullet and was actually proud of it or that another had married her kidnapper?! LOL! Good times! It was a brief break from the usual, and we resumed our meeting with newly formed smiles.

7. Thank someone. Who does not love being recognized for a job well done?! While you might not do it at every meeting, work it into the agenda as often as you can and in as authentic and sincere of a way as possible. Hard work deserves recognizing, and when you recognize it, you get more of it. And recognizing one's efforts in front of his colleagues could not be any better way to do it!

8. Assign action items. Now that we are done, what do we do? Ensure this question is answered because if it is not, then it was just a meeting for the sake of holding a meeting with nothing gained and no one any closer to achieving a goal. Throughout the course of the meeting, identify what needs to be done to reach the objectives you outlined at the meeting's start. Then once you come to a conclusion, invite volunteers to take on those action items, or have people in mind whom you know will know a bang-up, knock-out, outrageously amazing job. And, in your most sincere tone, tell them that you know that is the kind of performance you foresee—bang-up, knock-out, outrageously amazing work— and guess what. They will rise to the occasion.

DAY 11 SIZZLERS

1. When and where are you at your happiest? How can you create more opportunities like that for yourself?

    _____

    _____

    _____

2. When was the last time you reviewed your personal goals? How many of them and which ones will you reach by year's end?

    _____

    _____

    _____

3. How well do you protect your time and the time of others? Do you ensure the majority of your time is spent engaging in uplifting yourself and/or others?

    _____

    _____

    _____

4. How often do you hear from others? How often do you get advice and encouragement from your circle, and how often do you check-in with those close to you?

    _____

    _____

5. When was the last time you said "thank you" to someone? Is it time to show your appreciation for a colleague, friend, or relative for just being who they are? Who is it?

_____

_____

_____

_____

DAY 12
Five Actionable Strategies to be an Unforgettable Speaker
effective communication | presentation skills

Five actions are necessary if you want to give your audiences a different experience that will be unforgettable for all the right reasons. This goes for novice presenters, struggling presenters, and seasoned presenters alike. Here's exactly how to make your public and private presentations memorable, engaging, and blazing hot.

1. Tell them your HOW and your WHY, not your WHAT. Audience members want to know how you can help them be more powerful, more productive, better professionals, incredibly outstanding in all facets of their lives. They want to know why they should listen to you. It matters not to the audience what YOU know or what you do until you show them how you can help them with what THEY do! Blow off their socks by telling them how you bring about transformations and why the work you do is the best work in the world. You almost want to think about your elevator pitch here and selling yourself to the audience. Once you make it clear you are there to make a difference, then you have them in the palm of your hand. All that is left to do is to bring the content. Bring the heat!

2. Make it a conversation. It is assumed you are an expert because you have the microphone. Assume you also have experts in front of you, and let them show off! Turn your presentation into a conversation where you speak for only so long—bring the heat—then bring in other voices so you engage the audience and demonstrate your point of view isn't the only one in the room.

3. Steer away from sharing too many of your accomplishments. It can appear braggadocios, and it can alienate the audience, resulting in everyone having the impression you believe you are better than everyone assembled. When you shine the light on everyone else in the room, YOU shine! When you brag about a great question someone asked or praise someone for making an interesting contribution, when make the other person feel like the most important person in the room, then YOU become the most important person in the room.

4. Consistently, look and sound unstoppable.

Look and sound like the role you want to portray; establish your credibility; and capitalize on using the three pillars of persuasive speech, ethos, logos, and pathos.

Shoulders back, head up, eyes laser-focused; adopt these practices with your body language every single time you speak. Every single time no matter where you are and no matter to whom you speak. Eliminate the "uh's" and "um's" otherwise known as filler words. Make statements that sound certain, not flimsy. For instance, say, "I know," not "I think." Eliminate high-rising terminals or uptalk so every statement you make does not sound like a question. You must give the impression you are the most confident and powerful speaker there is, and when you do that, you will be unforgettable.

5. Give a call-to-action. After you present, move the audience to extend its thinking and its engagement so they remember you and your message well after you have finished speaking. Take your audience members from listening to acting, and when you do that, you inspire your listeners to do more, be more, and realize how incredibly dynamic they are. You ... YOU did that!

DAY 12 SIZZLERS

1. What is your "why"? What gets you out of bed each day? What makes you show up and shine for others?

   _____

   _____

   _____

2. Who is an expert in your network with whom you need to have a conversation? Who can you get on your calendar for meaningful dialogue where you learn from each other?

   _____

   _____

   _____

3. When was the last time you documented your accomplishments? Take time to identify and personally celebrate the wins you have scored in your personal life and in your professional life thus far this year.

   _____

   _____

   _____

4. Can you look use a communication makeover? How powerful do you look and feel when you speak? Is it

time to reevaluate how you project yourself to the world?

_____

_____

_____

5. What are three calls-to-action you can give people whenever you engage with them? What is an article you will recommend? A book you will suggest? A quote you love? How can you consistently move people to action?

_____

_____

_____

DAY 13
Could This Be the Key to Teaching Any Course with Passion and Enthusiasm?

audience-centric experience | effective communication | lecturing | presentation skills | student-centric experience

One of three situations is before you.

You have been assigned a course that is unequivocally one of your least favorite to teach.
OR
You are teaching the same course for the umpteenth time.

OR

It is your first time teaching. First. Time. Ever.

And believe it or not, all three of these educators are similarly positioned because you consciously think to yourself "I have to find a way to make it through this term and appear to effortlessly make it through without faltering or running out of steam for both my and the students' sake. How is THAT possible?!"

What you must know is it is entirely possible to make it an enjoyable and worthwhile experience for both you and your students. When you create passion, interest, and enthusiasm at the start of each class session, you have created an environment that motivates all assembled, and no matter your years or lack thereof of expertise, here are the four steps you take to smoothly make your way through the term with grace, determination, excitement, passion, and enthusiasm in both you and your students.

1. Provide information: If you take away nothing else from this post, remember this: The number one reason adults will listen to you is they know why they should listen to you. Let students know the purpose of the class session and what they will know or be able to do upon conclusion of the class session. Clarify how the current class session connects to the last class session and/or how it connects to the overall course. Explain how this one puzzle piece fits with the larger picture, referring to the student learning objectives, the course description, and/or the textbook content to clearly illustrate how this class session will contribute to moving students closer to mastery and what new knowledge or abilities they will have once class ends that they did not have when they stepped into your classroom.

2. Pump up the classroom: Students should know the benefits of the class session and why it should be important to them. This is intricately connected to the act of informing students. Recall the number one reason adults will listen to you ... there is an excitement when you realize you can enhance yourself, your performance, your potential on some level as a result of having done X.

Get students to crave what you have to give them.

If you convey how students will improve as a result of having spent their time engaged with you, their classmates, and the course content during a class session, then students cannot help but to bubble with excitement.

3. Pull in your students: Capture and hold fast students' attention with a compelling fact, a startling statistic, a tangential comment, a cartoon ... Give your honest reaction to the content. "I was not enthused at all about teaching this topic today, but then I got to thinking ...." Change your voice or use your body language to speak for you. Draw

111

them in so there is no way their attention can get diverted from what is occurring in that classroom.

4. Pass the microphone: Get students immediately talking, writing, and moving so they know your voice, ideas, and actions are not the only valid ones in the room. Consider a classroom assessment technique or any number of icebreakers to involve students in the conversation. And as you progress through the session, your students' levels of interest and involvement can become greater elevated with active lecturing.

Sure, this takes conscious thought and preparation, but there is always this alternative: walk in, say "hello," then painfully chalk-and-talk for 50 minutes, 120 minutes, or two or three hours.

Make the passionate and enthusiastic choice. You and your students will thank you for it.

DAY 13 SIZZLERS

1. What kind of information do you give others? How helpful is it? What changes should you make to ensure you give information that is consistently helpful and meaningful to your listeners?

   _____

   _____

   _____

2. In what ways do you show your excitement for what you do? How do you excite others either about what you do or what they do?

   _____

   _____

   _____

3. How well do you engage others? How well do you draw in your listeners with the language you use?

   _____

   _____

   _____

4. How well do you make conversations about the other person and less about you?

   _____

   _____

5. What passionate, enthusiastic choices will you make throughout the day today?

DAY 14
Do This, and You Will Know for Sure Your Class (or Your Meeting) Was Amazing!

audience-centric experience | effective communication | effective meetings | lecturing | presentation skills | student-centric experience

Why wait until the student opinion surveys are tallied or until your dean, department head, or program manager evaluates you to find out how well you perform as an educator? And better yet why let someone else tell you whether you are doing a good job?! Harness the power of self-evaluation to assess your superstar status at the front of that room! (And if you conduct meetings, this is just as relevant! Simply exchange "students," "class," and "lesson" for "meeting attendees, "meeting," and "content/agenda.")

How exactly is this done? Simple! Ask and answer these questions at the conclusion of class (or a meeting!):

- Did I start class in a way that immediately grabbed students' attention? Were they engaged within the first few minutes of class? What might I have them write, read, say, or do at the start of the next class session to transform them into active listeners and thinkers?

- How was my pacing? Were there points where I should not have moved as quickly because I needed to emphasize an important point? If so, then how can I deliver that information to students? Were there points where I moved too slowly?

- Did I check to ensure students understood the content? What new classroom assessment activities should I include to check for understanding? How can I get students to monitor their own learning?

- Did I make an effective use of the time? Were there any lulls? Were there missed opportunities? Did I inadvertently let a student monopolize a portion of the class session? How can I effectively change that the next time it occurs? Did *I* monopolize at points when I should not have done so?

- Were students engaged and involved? Was there student-to-faculty interaction? Student-to-student interaction? Student-to-content interaction? What activities should I omit or revise?

- Did I present the lesson well? If I was a student in this class, would I walk away understanding the concepts? Would it have been an enjoyable experience for me?

- How should I start the next class session? In what ways can I conduct an effective and efficient review and summary of the last class session? How can I use activities to connect content we have already covered with new content?

- What changes should I make the next time I teach this topic? Were there some portions of the lesson that will benefit from students discussing rather than from me discussing them? Are there other more effective examples I should use to better illustrate a point? Is there a different homework assignment I should make?

To be entirely clear, this does not have to be a formal event; print this checklist and post it in your workspace, so upon the conclusion of a class session, you can effortlessly evaluate your class performance.

Educators (and if you facilitate meetings or presentations, you are indeed an educator with an audience of students in front of you) who know student performance can be directly influenced by instructor performance are the educators who engage in ongoing assessment. They are also the ones who embrace this beautifully illuminating opportunity to design within themselves the educators they wish they had had before them when they were students.

Educators should assess their performance at least a couple of times a month, and at a minimum, conduct an assessment upon conclusion of the term as a means of reflection and preparation for the next term.

And in all honesty, it is not entirely unrealistic to conduct an assessment at the conclusion of every class or even at the conclusion of every week; you can always mentally review during your walk from the classroom to your workspace what worked well and that upon which could be improved … easy as that!

If you are the conscientious educator who sincerely wants to improve for the sake of students' success, who wants to be the most dynamic educator ever, then you can appreciate the strength in self-assessment, a supremely proactive move to confirm, without a doubt, your class session was amazing.

DAY 14 SIZZLERS

1. Do you start all of your engagements in ways that immediately grab others' attention? Do your eye contact and other body language make people want to lean in and hear more?

   _____

   _____

   _____

2. The responsibility of ensuring a message is understood falls on the speaker's shoulders, not the listener's shoulders. How well do you monitor whether others understand you?

   _____

   _____

   _____

3. What do you need to omit from your communication and the way you communicate? What do you need to add?

   _____

   _____

   _____

4. Think about the last conversation you had. How well did it go? What could you do differently?

   _____

_____

_____

5. Do you make it a practice to self-evaluate various aspects of your life? What needs your review and some adjustments?

_____

_____

_____

DAY 15
You Need to Give Active Lectures, and Here's Why!

audience-centric experience | effective communication | lecturing | presentation skills | student-centric experience

Typical or traditional lecturing is used to present information that is complex and difficult to understand, but lecturing also typically uses one-directional communication, providing for little to no input from the listener.

Wait a minute.

Did I get that right?!

If typical or traditional lecturing is used to present information that is complex and difficult to understand and if someone—like a student—hears new information via a lecture and it happens to also be complex and difficult to understand information, then one might have some questions along the way.

But!

Lecturing also typically uses linear communication with only the educator speaking while students listening, so we really are unsure of whether learning actually takes place because ... well ... it's ... lecturing ... and no one but the educator provides any input! " The main flaw in the linear model is that it depicts communication as a one-way process where speakers only speak and never listen. It also implies that listeners listen and never speak or send messages" (Models).

At this point, I am imagining trying to put a square peg in a round hole or trying to hammer a nail with a crescent wrench. In short, it simply does not work quite right.

Sure, there are benefits to lecturing if you have large amounts of content to cover or if you want to ensure the message and content deliver are focused and relatively free of most noise—psychological, physiological, physical, and semantic noise. However, if the goal is to deliver content and know learning took place, then consider active lecturing.

Active lecturing recognizes if information is complex and difficult to understand, then, the listener or learner is better positioned to reach full comprehension if the listener does more than just listen to the delivery of information.

As such, active lecturing uses a transactional communication model and takes lecturing and makes it come alive—makes it active!—and includes not only the objective material from a discipline or content matter but also infuses analogies, metaphors, similes, anecdotes, and examples representative of ideas and images that connect to students' background. Lecturing is the act of talking *at* learners; active lecturing is the act of having a conversation with learners.

So now the question is how exactly does active lecturing look? Read "You Need to Give Active Lectures, and Here's How to Do It!" to find out!

DAY 15 SIZZLERS

1. How can you ensure your communication uses more two-way processes?

   _____

   _____

   _____

2. What is a great analogy you like to use?

   _____

   _____

   _____

3. What are some of your favorite metaphors and similes?

   _____

   _____

   _____

4. What is an amazing personal story that you need to tell someone who has not yet heard it? What is the lesson the person will learn from your story?

   _____

   _____

   _____

5. How can you ensure you are not talking *at* people but that you are engaging in a conversation for the sake of both parties learning?

DAY 16
You Need to Give Active Lectures, and Here's How to Do It!

audience-centric experience | effective communication | lecturing | presentation skills | student-centric experience

Students learn more when *they* talk than when *we* talk.

Really?!

Yes.

A friend and colleague told me that several years back, and the first time I heard it, I was crushed. Deflated. The wind was sucked right out of my sails. You see, I'm the type of person who, if you give me the microphone and a stage, makes an incredible challenge for anyone else to get a word in edgewise. But then this begs the question of whether my goal in the classroom was to satisfy my id or satisfy my students' need and desire to extend learning.

Yes, it was time for me to pass the mic and take up active lecturing where I ensure I am not the one in the classroom doing the majority of the talking.

Active lecturing takes the standard lecture and makes it a conversation between the educator, the facilitator of learning, and the students. The educator lectures for a brief period of time, roughly five to fifteen minutes, paying attention to students' levels of engagement and attention, then students engage with and process that lecture material.

This engagement and processing can involve the educator asking an open-ended question related to the mini-lecture, having students collaborate in pairs or small groups, or completing some specific classroom assessment techniques before another five- to fifteen-minute lecture begins.

When best demonstrated, in addition to the objective content one would ordinarily deliver in a traditional lecture, active lecturing includes most—but ideally *all*—of the following components:

- an opening statement or activity that immediately excites, engages, and involves learners;
- chunked information where you deliver no more than five to fifteen minutes of content before providing an opportunity for learners to engage with the content and determine what it means for them and their learning via the use of a classroom assessment activity, for instance;
- effective use of educational technology, other visual aids, voice, and nonverbal communication;
- a strong, deliberate conclusion that reviews what learners should know as a result of the lecture, an opportunity for learners to demonstrate what the learned; and
- a list of action items to extend learning and prepare students for the next class session.

With active lecturing, educators make students a part of the conversation, and when they do so, they see students' levels of engagement, involvement, interest, interaction, and comprehension become propelled by the wind in everyone's sails.

DAY 16 SIZZLERS

1. Are you the type to monopolize the microphone? Do you talk so much until you forget to give others an opportunity to speak? What can you do differently going forward? How can you be more intentional about hearing others speak?

   _____

   _____

   _____

2. What kinds of follow-up questions can you ask people to demonstrate you are genuinely interested in learning about them?

   _____

   _____

   _____

3. What changes can you make to your use of technology to be a more effective communicator? Are there times when you should call rather than text? Schedule a video call instead of sending an email message?

   _____

   _____

   _____

4. How strongly do you conclude your interactions with others? Is there a lackluster "goodbye" or a sincere and memorable expression of support for and appreciation of the other person?

_____

_____

_____

5. What activities can you complete today to extend your learning and get your ready for another day of productivity?

_____

_____

_____

DAY 17
Improve Your Public Speaking With This Very Simple Everyday Change!
effective communication | presentation skills

A student in one of my online Communication courses once wrote he wanted to practice becoming more confident when he spoke to strangers. He was wondering just how he might be more relaxed when he talked to people he met for the first time. Was there any technique he could employ on a weekly or—let's get ambitious here! —even a daily basis?

And after a week of discussion on effective presentation techniques, I realized this was not an isolated concern. Several other students began to speak up (or type) about reservations they had when meeting persons for the first time and wanting to exude confidence in their language.

We arrived at this conclusion ...

You are constantly on a stage, and you make a presentation every single time you speak.

Think about it. Each time you communicate, there is a definite purpose in mind no matter the size of your audience: your intent is to inform, persuade, or entertain. And each time you present, each time you speak, you want to show up and be memorable. So why wait until you are in front of a big crowd to work on your confidence? Why wait until you have a microphone, getting ready to make a formal presentation, to sound and look confident?

The decision we made was, going forward, if you are on the phone, on a webinar, or in person, pretend you are making a presentation. That was the very simple everyday change you should make. Pretend the quality of what you say is being closely evaluated and that you will be given a rating afterwards for the effectiveness of your message. Okay. Okay. Okay.

That may seem like a bit of an intense way to look at it. So how about this?:

Whether you are talking to ...

the cashier at the local grocery store,
the teller at the bank,
the teacher at your child's school,
the attendant at the gas station,
the barista at the coffee shop,
the employee at the theatre,
*the waiter at a local eatery ...

stand (or sit) with your shoulders back; head up; eyes focused on the listener; using a clear voice, carefully chosen words, and proper gestures/nonverbal communication ...

For when you have your shoulders back, it tells your listener what you have to say is important.

When your head is up, it sends the message you are proud of what you have to say.

When your eyes are focused on your listener, it shows your attention is respectfully focused on him/her and him/her alone.

When your voice is clear and when you take charge of the words you selected, you show you care about ensuring the listener understands your message.

When you use proper gestures, then you demonstrate a passion for and confidence in your message; your entire body, mind, and heart are in what you say. And in most instances, your listener cannot help but to feel and sense that passion and confidence.

Be more conscious every time you speak, and see the difference. You all remember those exercises where you dressed professionally, then visited an establishment and observed how you were treated differently. This is similar to that. Observe how you are better able to hold your listener's attention as well as how much more confident you feel.

DAY 17 SIZZLERS

1. What does it mean for your message and your image when you speak with your shoulders back? How does it make you feel?

   _____

   _____

   _____

2. How does your confidence change when your head is up, looking into your listener's eyes when you speak?

   _____

   _____

   _____

3. How well does your voice communicate you care about your message being understood?

   _____

   _____

   _____

4. How well do you use your body when you speak? Does it communicate your passion to your listener? What will you do differently?

   _____

   _____

   _____

5. Watch and listen to others you regard as confident speakers. What do they do that you should also put into practice?

_____

_____

_____

DAY 18
The Biggest Communication Mistake Introverts Make

audience-centric experience | effective communication | personal branding | presentation skills

We are often inclined to believe extroverts are the more skilled presenters when compared to their introverted counterparts, but ... hold the phone.

While words appear to come more easily for extroverts who gain their energy from being around others, introverts are missing out if they (and others) believe they are not serious contenders as speakers. Assuming introverts are not gifted speakers is the one mistake introverts make and the dangerous misconception held by so many. Quite to the contrary, they may be even more talented on the mic than others. Here are three reasons why.

1. Introverts are incredibly self-aware, and this bodes well for their speaking. Before they utter a word, introverts carefully scrutinize their ideas, paying keen attention to the entire packaging of their messaging. They are not quick to get on a microphone without first carefully analyzing any combination of their appearance, nonverbal communication, and/or how they want their message to be received. As such, during impromptu moments when called upon to "say a few words," they are not eager to speak up *not* because they do not have anything to say; it is because they have not had ample opportunity to organize their thoughts and ensure they produce a quality message—even if it is only to say a few words.

They want to carefully script in their minds what they will say so when it is verbalized, there is little to no room for them to look or sound less than polished. Now, this is not to suggest extroverts are not sensitive to the quality of their messages; they simply require far less time to organize their thoughts and, they prefer speaking during *un*scripted moments. They are the ones who do not need a slide deck and can crush it! But because of introverts' inclination to examine and re-examine most of what they plan to say before they verbalize it, their self-awareness and acute attention to detail can result in them being quite talented during formal speaking engagements.

2. Introverts like to build their skills in private as opposed to jumping in feet first. This is particularly advantageous for introverts because they are comfortable being in a room alone and are, therefore, more likely to practice for their presentations in the one and only way one should ever practice, which is to deliver presentations all alone while out of sight of others and deliver the presentation full-out as if there *is* an audience watching.

A mistake many speakers make is mentally going through their presentations and calling it practice, but introverts are less likely to make this mistake.

By conducting a dress rehearsal in private and without distractions, they hear the words they plan to articulate in front of the live audience. Once you hear the words, see the gestures, and get a sense of the flow of the presentation, you know where to fix lulls, how to ensure the audience is engaged, and whether your message is on-track. Knowing all of this and, more importantly, addressing it during practice and well before showtime results in a presentation that is methodically and thoughtfully delivered with intention.

3. Introverts' preference for learning by listening intently, paying attention to others, and making discoveries through observation gives them a true advantage when they speak. If there is any guarantee with any presentation, it is that your audience *will* give you a reaction without saying a word. Introverts' astute attention to others' nonverbal communication and introverts' tendency to be great observers is a plus in the presentation environment because if they sense a positive vibe from the audience, then they know they are on the right trajectory; however, if the body language tells them otherwise, then they know they need to do or say something different and do or say it quickly to avoid losing the momentum they have built.

Rather than committing to delivering the message at all costs while ignoring any telltale signs of negativity from listeners, if and when placed in a scenario where multiple audience members appear less than satisfied with the message, introverts are better positioned to use these reactions to address audience needs. Introverts will assess their content and its delivery, then offer points of clarification or opportunities for the audience to provide feedback.

Simply put, if one is an introvert, it does not mean one is *not* destined to be an incredible speaker. Actually, an introvert may be quite the thoughtful and organized speaker

144

with a heightened sense of awareness of audience needs. Commonly held or widely accepted beliefs lead people to believe extroverts are the ones who are ideally positioned to give the best speaking performances; however, it's time for a paradigm shift because—let's be clear—introverts are wired to rock the mic just as well as—if not better than!—anyone else.

DAY 18 SIZZLERS

1. What did you learn about introverts?

   _____

   _____

   _____

2. What did you learn about extroverts?

   _____

   _____

   _____

3. What surprised you about yourself?

   _____

   _____

   _____

4. What about communication was confirmed for you?

   _____

   _____

   _____

5. What will you do differently when you communicate?

   _____

   _____

   _____

DAY 19
The Most Critical Starting Point for Being an Effective Communicator
audience-centric experience | effective communication

You show up in life everyday with every intention of being amazing and making a difference. And just as you feel like you are hitting your stride—maybe you're even ready to high-five everyone you encounter because you have had a pretty good day so far—it happens.

You bump heads with someone who doesn't quite "speak your language," who's unhappy about one thing or another You simply know it can turn your day all the way around. What do you do, and more importantly, how do you keep your cool?

Knowing the communication styles of others (while simultaneously knowing your own preference) is the starting point to effective communication.

There is a multitude of communication styles that come with a myriad of labels found in a variety of sources; in the interest of simplicity, four are covered herein.

1. Connection Seekers. These persons seek a sense of personal rapport with you and wants emotional acceptance before engaging in an extensive conversation. For thes persons, start with small talk. They want you to ask about the family, in what pursuits they engaged over the weekend, and they are doing personally. If you fail to show an interest in them and what matters to them, then they get the impression you do not care about them. In short, they like knowing that they matter.

2. Honesty Seekers. These are the ones who want to know or need to know what's being communicated is logical, that it makes sense, that it's accurate, that it fits with their current knowledge base or current set of facts. Do not try to pull fast ones on these individuals. As they listen to others, they think "Can I trust this?" and can spot puffery a mile away. Honesty Seekers have a tendency to lose respect for or get frustrated with you if you are not straightforward with the information you provide.

3. Results Seekers. Give Results Seekers the bottom line. These are the ones who just need to know that can they use what you give. "How can I take this information and do something with it?" or "What's the bottom line?" is the question that constantly runs through their minds as someone speaks. They want information that's practical and that has utility. As such, small talk is not of great interest to them, and they can get frustrated with someone who rambles or who, from their point of view, talks just for the sake of filling silence.

4. Energy Seekers. They do not mind taking risks because they do not see them as risks—that which should be feared—but they see them in a positive light—as opportunities. They want to enter into discoveries, try new adventures, share energy with others. Energy Seekers think big picture and love exploring the possibilities. They constantly think "Why not?!" and "Let's do this!"

DAY 19 SIZZLERS

1. What did you learn about yourself and your preferred communication style?

    _____

    _____

    _____

2. What did you learn about the communication styles of others?

    _____

    _____

    _____

3. What surprised you about one of the communication styles?

    _____

    _____

    _____

4. Is there a communication theory for which you received confirmation or validation? What is it?

    _____

    _____

    _____

5. Going forward, what will you do differently in your communication with others?

DAY 20
Mistakes to Avoid When You Communicate with Those Who Do Not Communicate Like You

audience-centric experience | effective communication

When others have the same interests as you—reading material, athletic pursuits, hobbies—this common ground makes it easier to engage. It's no different when you communicate; however, we can use these preferences to choose who's in our book clubs, on our sports teams, and in our circle of friends, but we cannot, based on preferences, choose to whom we speak. In essence, you have to communicate with everyone regardless of whether that person shares your preferred style of communicating.

Each person needs a different experience when communicating, which requires you to stretch—get out of your communication style comfort zone—and know what mistakes to avoid and recognize what others need.

Connection Seekers. Because they often seek connections more than anything else in communication, they are mistakenly seen as being passive or as pushovers, which couldn't be further from the truth. They can stand their ground if need be, but it's not how they prefer to use their energy. They want to get to know others, and they want others to get to know them. Especially in business, they believe in relationships more than transactions. For them, it's the relationships they build with prospects and customers that will lead to transactions.

Honesty Seekers. Even if it's difficult or grim information, they would rather you be direct and upfront with the information than hold back or try to sugar-coat it to make it sound better. Watering-down details or skirting issues with Honesty Seekers only makes matters worse when communicating with them. Come with a written plan, cite reputable sources, and be as honest and transparent as you can no matter the news you have to give. Honesty Seekers can be seen as blunt, too direct, rude, or impatient, but they simply need you to get to the point so they can move on to offering solutions or the next item on their agendas.

Results Seekers. For Results Seekers, money is time, and time is money. Do not waste their time with insignificant details, and they deem insignificant details as those details that will not get them closer to a goal. Skip the details, and do not build up to a climax. If a Results Seeker asks a close-ended question, then answer with a concise response. Offer explanations only if the Result Seeker asks for explanations. Like Honesty Seekers, Result Seekers can also be seen as blunt or impatient. They can be seen as uncaring or harsh, but too many details can lead to frustration or confusion. They want to take the most direct path to get to answers. A, B, C, and D may be involved with getting to E; however, if only A and D are necessary to achieve arriving at D, then that is all they need. They focus on keeping everything in forward motion, and if too much time is spent on minor details, it takes from them energy that they would rather put toward arriving at solutions.

Energy Seekers. With Energy Seekers, show up as the best version of yourself where you look, sound, and act like you are excited to give the information. For Energy Seekers, their attitude is if you do not care and are not enthusiastic about your message, then why should they care or be enthusiastic. They can be mistaken for being over-the-top or "too much." When you engage with an Energy Seeker, you may be tempted to say to yourself "You're at a 10, and I need you to dial things back to about a 5." Energy Seekers are not drawn to you and have a hard time hearing—literally and figuratively—what you say if you sound bored, annoyed, exhausted, or if the message you give is more of the same or is a run-of-the-mill regurgitation of details. With Energy Seekers, they need you to look alive! They need you to come with it. If you want them to rally behind you and support your mission, then you have to speak with vitality and vigor, and passion.

The greatest takeaway here is no one communication style is better than the other one. They are preferences, and the more you know about how people like to communicate, the better equipped you are to match others' energy and give them what they need when you speak.

DAY 20 SIZZLERS

1. What mistakes do people make when communicating with you?

   _____

   _____

   _____

2. What mistakes have you made when communicating with those who do not have the same communication style as you?

   _____

   _____

   _____

3. Going forward, what will you do differently when communicating with others?

   _____

   _____

   _____

4. With which communication style is it most difficult for you to interact, and why??

   _____

   _____

   _____

5. For the communication style that is easiest for you, what changes will you make to be even more effective?

_____

_____

_____

DAY 21
Three Incredibly Easy Ideas to Keep Learning (and Presenting) Hot!

audience-centric experience | effective communication | effective meetings | presentation skills

Most people have quirks when they present. And I'm sure, although I have put forth great effort to be aware of quirks and eliminate them, I have one, or two, or three, or ...

As a matter of fact, I recall several years back—somewhere around 2012 or so—I collaborated with a friend and colleague to facilitate a workshop in the Denver, Colorado area, and his use of the phrase "what-not" apparently caught my attention because I did not realize until after the workshop and while reading one participant's feedback on her survey that I had picked up on his use of that phrase and had incorporated it into the last two sessions I presented at the workshop! She had actually sat and counted the number of times I had used it! *gasp* (And to be honest, I recalled, while I was presenting, seeing this particular person in the audience snickering at times that was obviously out of context. I ignored it at the time, thinking if there was anything relevant to share, then she would do so. It was all starting to come together ... LOL!)

But my goodness! I could not believe it! In retrospect, I had caught the "what-not" bug and was using the phrase like it was going out of style! I had never done that before! (At least I do not recall doing so!) My colleague's use of it subconsciously caused me to use it.

This is what happened: We converge with interlocutors that we like or that we want to like us. This colleague who is also a friend and is one with whom I have a great professional relationship, so based on this phonetic and social selectivity, it was natural I would pick up on one of his catch phrases and use it myself or that I would ... converge with an interlocutor!

As I thought about the workshop and this participant's feedback, I could not help but to wonder (and worry!) if her focus on counting my "what-not's" interfered with her actual learning. I wondered if my temporary presentation misstep consumed her and subsequently caused her to lose an opportunity to learn. What had I done?!

The greatest goal of any presentation is to ensure learning takes place and that participants take action based on what they learn.

This got me thinking ... What plans can I put in place beforehand to provide my audiences with the most awesome learning experience possible? I came up with three ideas.

1. Keep it active. Provide multiple opportunities for participants to hear from themselves and others via writing and discussions. That way, they have opportunities to think about the substance of what you have presented and process it means for the work they do. (And, that way, your voice is not the only one in the room!)

2. Conduct brief, on-the-spot self-assessments. While the audience is engaging in an activity, conduct a mental recap of the last several minutes of the presentation. Were there quirks or missteps that should be avoided going forward? Did you ensure you used power words as opposed to wimpy words? How well did you handle audience questions? If you have them engaging in conversations, roam around the room to show interest and to model good facilitation skills, while you conduct your own internal conversation with yourself.

3. Check the temperature. Pause and ask the audience if we need to go in a different direction or keep moving on the planned route while keeping in mind your objectives. Whatever change you make, ensure it aligns with what you want to accomplish overall, and avoid changing just for the sake of making the audience happy. A change in direction could mean stopping to consider alternatives to what has been presented and examine whether there are missing points need to be covered. This is not expected and is not the norm for a presentation and, as such, will certainly break the pattern of what their brains expect and helps learning to not be cold and boring but rather hot and relevant!

Day 21 SIZZLERS

1. What quirks do you have when you speak?

   _____

   _____

   _____

2. Do those quirks add to or detract from your message's effectiveness? If so, then what should you do differently?

   _____

   _____

   _____

3. What phrases have you heard from others that are particularly powerful that you can add to your speaking repertoire?

   _____

   _____

   _____

4. How will keeping listeners active, conducting on-the-spot self-assessments, and checking the temperature improve your speaking game?

   _____

   _____

   _____

5. What can you put in place beforehand to provide your audiences with the most awesome learning experiences possible?

_____

_____

_____

DAY 22
Four Steps to Cut Your Presentation Prep Work in Half
audience-centric experience | effective communication | presentation design | presentation skills

Does this sound like you?:

- "I have so much information to cover until I don't know where to start, what to do, or how to do it!"

- "My presentations are pretty good, but I want them to be great! I need a systematic plan so I'm not just going through the motions, muddling through."
- "What will make a difference with my audience?! What will draw them in, and—and most importantly!!!—what will get everyone to buy what I'm selling?!" (literally or figuratively speaking)

What you must know is it is entirely possible to make your presentation an enjoyable and worthwhile experience for both you and your audience without it being more work for yourself.

Here are the four steps you take to smoothly make your way through preparing for your presentations with grace, determination, excitement, passion, and enthusiasm. Make this a consistent practice—resolve this is what you will do every time you prepare a presentation—and you will joyfully break free of the presentation preparation nightmare and cut your prep work by 50%.

1. Give the audience real information! Remember this: The number one reason adults will listen to you is they know why they should listen to you. Immediately clarify for the audience what everyone will know or be able to do upon conclusion of the presentation. Clarify how your presentation/product/topic connects to the last presentation/meeting and/or how it connects to the work everyone does. Explain how this one puzzle piece (your presentation) fits with the larger picture; clearly illustrate how your session will contribute to moving listeners closer to personal/professional goals and what new knowledge or abilities they will have once the presentation concludes— knowledge or abilities they did not have when they stepped into your presentation.

2. Decide exactly how you will excite everyone. Your listeners' heart rates need increasing, and this is done by giving them the benefits of the presentation and why it has any importance to them. Why should they care? Seriously. What is going to make their eyebrows go up? What is going to put them on the edges of their seats. This is intricately connected to the act of informing listeners. Recall the number one reason adults will listen to you … there is an excitement when you realize you can enhance yourself, your performance, your potential on some level as a result of having done X. Get your audiences to crave what you have to give with them! If you convey how some aspect of listeners' lives or work will be better as a result of having spent their time engaged with you and your content during a presentation, then listeners cannot help but to bubble with excitement.

3. Draw them in with your excitement. Capture and hold fast listeners' attention with your passion. Give your honest reaction to the content. Show that you love it. Find a way to love it if need be! Change your voice or use your body language to speak for you. Pull them into your world and have them feel what you're feeling so there is no way their attention can get diverted from what is occurring at the front of that room.

4. Make it a two-way street. – Get listeners immediately talking, writing, and/or moving so they know your voice, ideas, and actions are not the only valid ones in the room. Audience members learn more, lean in more, are better inclined to act as you want them to act if the idea feels like it came from them. Did you catch that? If they are involved ... if the presentation is a two-way street ... if their voices are heard, then they are more likely to get on your bandwagon and pick up what you're putting down.

Sure, this takes conscious thought and preparation, but there is always this alternative: walk in, say "hello," then painfully subject your audience to 15, 30, or even 60 or more minutes of a sit-and-get session.

Once you resolve to commit to these four practices—once you get this down-pat and perform this on a consistent basis—your presentation prep work is much further along and so is your audience's desire to act!

DAY 22 SIZZLERS

1. Why should others listen to you? Why should people give you their attention when you speak?

   _____

   _____

   _____

2. What knowledge do you have that others crave?

   _____

   _____

   _____

3. How can you excite your listeners?

   _____

   _____

   _____

4. What can you do to keep all eyes on you?

   _____

   _____

   _____

5. What can you do to ensure the voices of your listeners are always heard?

   _____

   _____

   _____

DAY 23
The VERY BEST Ways to Conclude Any Class Session
audience-centric experience | lecturing |
student-centric experience

Regardless of your discipline, use these techniques to conclude class in a way that is meaningful and that sets-up students for success. These strategies take you beyond making a homework assignment and saying "I'll see you next class."

These strategies reiterate for your students your commitment to their learning and your goal to extend the conversation beyond the classroom's four walls.

1. Be intentional with your questioning. Devote one-sixth of your class time to questions. This can occur throughout the lecture or at the end of lecture. As opposed to asking if there are any questions, ask very specific questions that give you an assessment of whether learners understood the material presented. Look at the objectives you have for the class session. What did you identify as that which learners will know or be able to do upon the conclusion of the class session? Use those objectives as well as what you covered to create more meaningful questions.

2. Propose study questions. Use lectures to set up problems or propose study questions for discussion that learners are expected to prepare for lab or the next class meeting. End the lecture with a provocative question. Begin the lab or the next class session with a discussion of that problem or issue. Use this when assigning readings; pose a provocative question to which learners will learn the answer upon completing the reading.

3. Give a one-question quiz. At the end of your lecture, or at any other appropriate stopping point, give learners a one-question "quiz," based on the material just covered in the class. Ask them to answer the question collectively. Leave the room so that they can discuss the question for five or ten minutes. Then return and have them report their answers; discuss with them the reasons for their choices.

4. Have students write a one-minute paper at the end of class. In this exercise, learners write down what they consider the main point of the class or the main question they still have as they leave. Select questions to use to begin the next class session, or you instruct learners to bring them to the next class session or lab.

DAY 23 SIZZLERS

1. How much do you like your current questioning strategy when you are in conversation or when you make a presentation? How thought-provoking are your current questions?

   _____

   _____

   _____

2. What can you do to be more intentional about the questions you ask others when you are in conversation?

   _____

   _____

   _____

3. How will more intentionality behind your questions impact your presentations?

   _____

   _____

   _____

4. In what ways will both you and your audiences benefit from your improved questioning strategies?

   _____

   _____

   _____

5. What provocative questions can you pose to your audiences that will extend the conversation beyond your presentation? How can you get your audience to continue thinking about your content long after your presentation has concluded?

_____

_____

_____

DAY 24
Do You Annoy People With the Sound of Your Voice?

effective communication | personal branding |
presentation skills

I know this is going to sound really really lame, but one of my favorite—I'm talking about FA-VO-RITE!—topics is pitch. You know ... as in the pitch of your voice. When it comes to building confidence, this is your starting point. This is how you sound confident every single time you speak. Every. Single. Time. When you work on the pitch of your voice and consciously project it with assertiveness, each time you open your mouth, everyone knows to sit up and pay attention.

This is the deal: Men tend have an advantage over women in this area because their voices are already at a lower pitch, so they already sound commanding and sure. For women, a downfall can be a higher pitched voice, which does not resonate with people and can cause our messages to be discounted. The lower your pitch, the higher your confidence. Remember that.

But before you think you have to start channeling your inner Barry White, Sean Connery, or James Earl Jones ... before you start to think I'm suggesting a woman needs to sound like a man, hear (or read) me out. Women's voices are supposed to be gentler. They are supposed to have a different tone. Absolutely.

But take note that when women's voices have lower pitches, women are better respected.

People are more inclined to listen to you, more inclined to believe you, and more inclined to have a better rapport with you.

Over the years, I've noticed when women have brief conversational encounters with people, they tend to raise the pitch of their voices and/or speak with a nasally sound. I hear it quite often during networking events, when I call a company, or at restaurants when greeted by a hostess or waitress. And I hear it when women begin and end their presentations.

Also avoid sounding nasally. This is when you tighten your throat and talk through your nose. For some reason, women often subconsciously do this—again—thinking it makes them sound less threatening and more pleasant. It doesn't. It's all well-meaning. It's all in an effort to sound friendly and accommodating; however, it can actually make you sound less confident and somewhat artificial.

In short, if your pitch is too high or nasally, then your voice can sound irritating or immature, which can cause people to discount you and your message, and it can cause your confidence to be low when you speak. When you use your normal speaking voice and your pitch is just right, you sound sure of yourself and, consequently, you *feel* sure of yourself.

DAY 24 SIZZLERS

1. Listen to a recording of yourself speaking. How confident does your voice sound?

   _____

   _____

   _____

2. What impression do you believe your voice gives others?

   _____

   _____

   _____

3. What impression do you want your voice to give others?

   _____

   _____

   _____

4. Think of someone who has a powerful voice. What is it about that person's voice that you like so much?

   _____

   _____

   _____

5. Aside from paying attention to the tone of your voice, what else can you do so people are more inclined to listen to and believe you?

_____

_____

_____

DAY 25
Three Secrets to Get Educators to Adopt Edtech

edtech presentations | effective communication |
presentation skills

My time spent teaching in higher ed and providing
professional development, faculty development, and
educational technology strategy for a content provider—you
know ... we called them publishing companies before the
digital evolution—uniquely positions me to view sales from
both sides of the desk.

Educators want what will impact learning, and sales force members are ready and willing to provide just that. However, for an educator who has been teaching a certain way for decades or if even for only a few short years, change can be uncomfortable.

This post is prompted by a conversation with an edtech sales professional. I told her about these three ideas, and she repeatedly responded with a contemplative "Interesting ...." Let's see if you have a similar reaction.

1. The "Students use it, so you should, too!" pitch is ineffective.

This approach suggests to an educator what he/she currently does is not working or his/her efforts to education today's student are futile. No one wants to hear that! Imagine your response if someone told you that you should engage in one activity or another because others are already doing so. REALLY?! On the other hand, if one told you the power you could have, the impact you could create, the change you could effect with that activity, then you might reconsider. Rather than identify a tech tool then try to force-fit it into the educator's world, find out the educator's pain point, then identify a tech tool that speaks to it. This places the educator in the position of being a forward-thinking leader who used technology to solve a problem as opposed to a blind follower.

2. When the microwave was invented, did we all stop cooking on stoves?

Yes, technology is the fuel that makes us go faster, work more efficiently, and cover wider ground. Should we force everyone to abandon tools of yesterday for the new, bright, and shiny invention of today? An immediate all-or-nothing/everything-must-be digital approach may not work for all educators; and while it may be inconvenient and more costly to oblige an educator who insists on still owning a hardcover copy of the book even after you've artfully sold him/her on digital, know your efforts were not in vain. The fact he/she is open to the idea technology for use by students suggests ... well ... he/she is open to the idea of technology! In due time, you can move him/her, too.

3. You would not put someone who's afraid of driving behind the wheel of a Ferrari.

Trying new ideas—like edtech—can be scary or down-right terrifying! Scaffold educators with manageable steps. Start by having the educator test (drive) the technology but in a discipline other than the one in which he/she teaches. Follow-up by asking how effective was his/her personal learning experience. Another idea is start with only one of

185

the educator's sections that adopts a tech tool, then bring other sections on-board the next term.

(I can take no credit for the Ferrari analogy; a big "thank you" goes to my colleague and successful publishing sales expert, Cheryl Stevens. At the time, I told her, "Don't be surprised if you hear or see me use that somewhere. You've been warned!" Hey ... I'm a woman of my word!)

DAY 25 SIZZLERS

1. What makes change uncomfortable?

2. What can you do in your presentations to position your listeners to be forward-thinking?

3. Do you have an all-or-nothing approach in your presentations? Do you position your ideas as the only ones to consider? What should you do differently?

4. How impactful would it be to combine your ideas with the audience's ideas?

5. What small steps can you encourage your audiences to take that will move them closer to putting ideas in place on a larger scale?

_____

_____

_____

DAY 26
Will Yoga Pants Make You Look Credible?
personal branding

Attire can be such a touchy subject, but you know me. I have to go there.

One consistent message you will hear (or read) from me is the importance of wearing *sleeves and wearing dark colors when/if you want to be taken seriously. I recognize dark blues, grays, and browns and black can be considered drab and boring, and I know during the summertime, sleeves or a suit can be the last thing you want to wear. Know this:

I need you to be seen and remembered as a put-together, serious professional who knows his/her stuff, and upon first glance at you, that's the impression others immediately get.

This is not to say you cannot put a splash of color in your outfit, e.g., a dark suit and a sensational blouse or some really interesting shoes can do the trick to make you feel like you are not just another suit in the room. And when it comes to the heat, unless you are making a two-hour presentation while standing outdoors under the blazing sun, then wearing sleeves while traversing from the parking lot to the building where you will present is entirely doable.

People will make a judgment call about you within the first seven seconds of meeting you, and matters are compounded when women are so incredibly critical of each other. (Why in the world do we do that to each other?!) We size up each other's outfits and make all sorts of assumptions about each other before a person even gets a chance to utter a word. Err on the side of caution and control your message with conservative attire because a well-put-together outfit that screams "She's in control" can only boost your credibility.

Now, I recognize there are some industries where lighter colors and more contemporary or unconventional attire is acceptable ... it's almost expected. (Think of the fashion or entertainment industry.) The expectation is you will not blend in the crowd but that you will express your creativity and individuality. Even then know the impression you want to give. Are you well groomed? Are your clothes tailored and best suited for your body type? Do the colors complement you?

Every single thing you do is a representation of your brand whether it's a company brand or your personal brand. Sure, layered tops, yoga pants, and scarves may be trendy for the moment, but what message does this outfit send to the audience if you need to be taken seriously or if you are expecting prospects to spend serious dollars with you, especially if you are not conducting a sales presentation on the new yoga mats your company just designed? Before stepping out the door, ask yourself, "What is the one word I want people to associate with me within the first seven seconds they see me?"

Your attire should not upstage an event or the audience members seated before you. Dress about a step above your audience members. For instance, if the audience is likely to show up wearing a mix of business and/or business casual attire, then you should dress in business attire. Business casual is not an option in this instance. And ensure accessories are kept modest and tasteful. You want to be remembered for your business sense and not for your lacy top or your Rolex watch. Instead, stand out with your personality and the amazing presentation you provide!

Naturally, if you make a presentation in a formal or black-tie setting, then you wear a formal that flatters you. If you are speaking at a company picnic, then leave the suit at home. (And the yoga pants need to stay in the closet, too.)

*Sleeveless tops make me think of building sandcastles at the beach, sipping tasty drinks poolside, or playing racquetball at a fabulous rec center ... sleeveless tops and dresses on women do not scream "professional." If you want to look credible, cover those shoulders, and rock it out. And besides, you can always take off the jacket the minute you're done. You've got this!

DAY 26 SIZZLERS

1. When people see you, what do you want them to think? In short, what is your personal brand?

_____

_____

_____

2. How well does your attire align with your company or personal brand?

_____

_____

_____

3. What impression do you want others to have of you if they only get to see you and not hear you speak?

_____

_____

_____

4. What's next for you in your profession? Do you want to move into another position or win a promotion? If so, then how well does your appearance communicate that desire?

_____

_____

_____

5. What changes, if any do you need to make to your attire and how you project yourself to the world?

_____

_____

_____

DAY 27
A Reality from Both Sides of the College Classroom Desk
student-centric experience

"College is not the thirteenth grade."

Can you remember hearing that sentence or one similar to it being announced at freshman orientation when you were a student, starting out on your college journey? You may have facetiously gasped in surprise. You may have rolled your eyes at the absurdity of the statement. (You were seventeen- or eighteen-years-old at the time, so that would have been totally normal, right?) You may have laughed it off.

Or you may have had a moment of clarity, and a lightbulb popped on. And right then and there, the epiphany comes:

You are now a college student swimming in an ocean far larger than the kiddie pool at your former high school; you are among students who are older, more experienced, possibly even brighter than you—so you think, and there are educators who expect you to come to class with more than a shiny, red apple and a smile.

You are immediately expected to know the norms and behaviors characteristic of a successful college student, but … well … it seems you were absent on the day they covered all of that in high school.

College freshmen are new on the job, and matters are further complicated when students enroll in an online course but have never had to learn in a virtual environment.

(Remember while it is true younger generations of students grew up with technology and know how to use it for personal reasons, they are not adept at using it for academic purposes.) Education has been done to them for thirteen years prior to arriving in college (kindergarten plus 12 grades of elementary and secondary school); they may not have had relationships with instructors where they could question much of anything. And for the most part, a student's progress was discussed between the parent and the teacher with little to no input or feedback from the student. For the most part, the parents and the teachers were the ones who had the conversations about effective and ineffective learning, the resources available, not the students and the teachers.

And then they get to college where all of a sudden, we immediately insist they, in the midst of their own personal mindsets, take charge of their learning, that they claim ownership of their education, identify and use academic resources, and serve as the primary contact with their instructors in accordance with the Family Educational Rights and Privacy Act (FERPA). However, this is entirely new to them. Subconsciously, educators can forget the effective transition from high school to college amounts to more than a student applying to, being accepted by, and enrolling in courses at an institution; the transition is not the equivalent of flipping a switch.

So this is the reality and a loose definition of the challenge. Now what do you do to address it? Read "This is What College Students Wish Educators Would Tell Them" to answer that question.

DAY 27 SIZZLERS

1. Based on what you now know about what it takes to succeed, what would you tell your 18-year-old self?

   _____

   _____

   _____

2. What lessons have you learned through trial and error that you wish had been directly taught to you?

   _____

   _____

   _____

3. What would have been different if those lessons had been taught directly?

   _____

   _____

   _____

4. How are you stronger because you had to learn the lessons on your own?

   _____

   _____

   _____

5. What lessons will you pass down to those who are up and coming in your personal and/or professional circle?

_____

_____

_____

DAY 28
This is What College Students Wish Educators Would Tell Them
student-centric experience

Educators find themselves insisting new students make the leap from high school to the post-secondary environment and behave differently, more responsibly, more seriously with regard to their academic ambitions once they enter onto college campuses. As such, educators can also find themselves in a quandary, convening in the faculty workroom or in online educator forums, commiserating with colleagues over new students not rising to the occasion as quickly as they would prefer.

By the time they reach college doors, though, students have been children much longer than they have been adults, and many may have come from the school of thought that children are to be seen and not heard when it comes to engaging in the learning process and education on a whole.

How, then, can educators expect thirteen years of habits and expectations to become undone and reworked during the course of, say, one new student orientation session?

Here are three recommendations for educators to help students successfully make the leap and make it in a timely fashion:

1. Encourage students to take a college success course if your campus offers one, or incorporate elements of college success programs into your syllabus and course. Consider what you believe are the attitudes and behaviors necessary for success on the collegiate level, drawing from personal experiences and other sources, and draft a list to provide to students. It might be punctuality, effective verbal and written communication skills, or even the benefits of regularly exercising and/or consuming a healthy diet. Consistently provide students with resources—websites, podcasts, articles, videos, on-campus workshops—where they can learn more about the recommendations you make.

2. Hold open and honest conversations with students both collectively as a class and in one-on-one settings. Explain to students the behaviors, attitudes, and habits they form now are in preparation for being self-sufficient adults who serve as leaders in their personal and professional communities. Bear in mind, though, the manner in which you hold these conversations will determine how well the messages are received and, subsequently, implemented. Remember there is a big difference between talking down or working hard to make a point of what students do not know versus guiding them with encouraging words, sharing what they need to know.

3. Draw from a variety of resources, including your own experiences, and give students a list of characteristics of successful college students plus a list of the characteristics of struggling college students. Years of being in the world of work can create a gap that causes educators to forget what their college lives may have been like and the fact they possess hidden gems. I know for me, I wish I had consciously known writing and reading were my learning preferences when I first arrived to college; I knew I was one of those students who had to take notes and who had to have her textbook as a reference while the professor lectured, but I never knew *why* that was the case. To that end, one characteristic of successful students might be "they know how they learn best and operate accordingly" versus a characteristic of struggling students might be "they are unsure of whether reading, writing, listening, or manipulating objects works best for them when they learn."

DAY 28 SIZZLERS

1. What attitudes and behaviors are necessary for your personal and professional success?

2. Of what resources—websites, podcasts, articles, videos, conferences, workshops—should you avail yourself?

3. What are your goals for the next month, and how are you preparing yourself now to meet those goals?

4. What open, honest conversation do you need to have with yourself right now?

5. What are the characteristics of a successful professional in your industry? Which of those characteristics do you already have? Which do you need to hone or develop?

_____

_____

_____

DAY 29
The Most Effective Networking Strategies You'll Ever Need

effective communication | networking | personal branding

Even in today's digital society where so much networking takes place online, face-to-face networking events are superior to virtual connections. The latter allow for more memorable connections, but when you attend networking events, sometimes interacting with others can make you feel like anything but a boss.

When you network, you make a presentation, and no matter your industry or your position, you are an ambassador for your company and, most importantly, for yourself.

Here are the five most effective networking strategies you will ever need.

1. Tell your story. A friend of mine told me she once attended a conference where she knew a particular decision-maker she wanted to meet and with whom she wanted to do business would be in attendance also. She spotted that person, walked up, began her pitch, but was met with the recommendation that she go online to complete the vendor application. The average person would have said, "Okay. Sure." However, this friend is far from average. She said, "I hear you, but first, allow me to tell you my story."

Less than a minute later, the professional said, "You've got my attention, and I want to do business with you."
What happened?

She told her story of going from being a struggling college student who worked multiple jobs to becoming an employee who was suddenly laid-off to deciding to follow her passion and become her own boss. However, it wasn't just a story, but it was what the story demonstrated to the decision-maker:

- The decision-maker saw her ability to be vulnerable and honest; her integrity was undeniable.
- The decision-maker got a sense of her work ethic and mindset; it was clear she believes in getting the job done
- The decision-maker would have a hard time forgetting her because she stood out and made herself memorable.

Tell your zero-to-champion stories, and dare to not look, sound, or act like everyone else in the same industry or space.

2.   Be a matchmaker, and seek-out other matchmakers. Everybody knows somebody. If you have your eye on a specific power partner, ask those in your circle if they know anyone who knows the person—and then ask for an introduction, and this turns into a warm lead, which is more effective than a cold email or phone call.

Be careful, though, not to take advantage of a situation, and commit to return the favor as much as possible. A first step to take is to build your own network so you can indeed reciprocate and to increase the likelihood that others will want to refer you because you have demonstrated you are a serious professional who understands and respects the power of a strong network.

3. Aim to give more than you receive. Professionals oftentimes approach networking events with the attitude of "What can I get out of who's in the room?" A better approach is to think "What can I give to everyone who's in the room?"

If you can help someone build on an idea, identify a solution, grow a plan, then you are doing more than collecting business cards, but you are establishing a relationship. People do business with and refer those they like. When you demonstrate you are not there to just take but that you are there to invest in the businesses and pursuits of others, you demonstrate your value. Aim to start and/or conclude conversations with "What can I do to help you?"

4. Be ready with a lesson, and be ready to be a learner. What is a piece of professional advice you received that resonated with you? What compelling book or article have you read that made an impression on you? What presentation have you heard or what conference did you recently attend that had you talking about it long after the event concluded? Give a mini-lesson of sorts on an experience that made an impression on you, then ask follow-up questions that puts you in the position to learn from the other person. For example ...

- "Let me tell you about this piece of advice that is, quite frankly, one of the best pieces of advice I've ever heard! ...." Follow-up with "What advice have you gotten that won't leave you?"

- "There's a book I'm reading right now that I simply cannot put down. Here's why ...." Then follow-up with "What book have you come across that's a page-turner?"

- "I attended a presentation at XYZ conference, and that session alone was worth the price of admission. This is one thing the presenter said/did that made the presentation so memorable ...." Finally, follow-up with "Have you had a similar experience? What are some professional conferences you would recommend?"

5. See beyond the networking event. Make it a point to continue your conversations beyond the networking event, and here's why. If someone walks away with nothing but your business card and no follow-up from you, then the likelihood of that professional being able to promote you and what you do is slim. However, if the person becomes a friend and is someone with whom you connect on a regular basis, then the person is more inclined to support you and keep an ear out for opportunities that fit your industry.

DAY 29 SIZZLERS

1. What is your zero-to-champion story?

2. What can you do to ensure you do not look, sound, or act like everyone else in your industry or space?

3. What steps can you take to build your network?

4. How can you approach or conclude conversations in the spirt of giving?

5. What steps can you put in place to ensure you consistently follow-up with those you view as valuable new contacts?

DAY 30
Have Students Do This One Thing to Positively Impact the Trajectory of Their Success
lecturing | student-centric experience

You have 50 or 80 minutes at a time and a room full of students. (If you're a speaker/trainer/sales or marketing pro, you have a room full of professionals. Read on, and get the bonus messages.) You do your best to reach them with active learning techniques, the effective use of technology, and/or meaningful assessments and questions. You almost feel like you have to be a superhero to ensure everyone gets it ... to ensure everyone is engaged ... to ensure everyone is positioned to see utility in the information you provide.

Put some of the responsibility on your students' shoulders, and have them do this one thing—regardless of their major and regardless of what you teach—to positively influence the trajectory of their academic success.

That one thing is ...

Help students discover which type of learner each one is. To informally help a student discover which type of learner he/she is, you can ask a student to consider how he/she would go about purchasing a car: Would he/she want to read descriptions and details about the car? If so, then this student is likely a visual learner. Would he/she want to talk with others who have previously owned the car to get their opinions, or would he/she listen very carefully and closely to the salesperson's explanation regarding the car? If so, then this student is likely an auditory learner. Would he/she conduct research and create charts to compare statistics and data about the car? If so, then this student may have a reading/writing preference for learning. Or would he/she want to test drive the car, look under the hood, and kick the tires? If so, then this student may be a kinesthetic learner. Depending on the one option the student would be most likely to do, that can determine how he/she likes to take in information and how he/she likes to produce or deliver information; in short, it can determine the kind of learner he/she is.

To formally help a student discover which type of learner he/she is, direct him/her to complete any one of a number of online assessments:

1. EducationPlanner, a self-proclaimed one-stop career and college planning website, offers a 20-question learning style assessment.

2. The VARK Questionnaire has students respond to items to determine how they learn best. This is my favorite assessment as it provides the student with help sheets that offer guidance on how to fully use individual learning styles to maximize success.

BONUS MESSAGE: What if you have professionals and not students in the audience? Assume your listeners represent all of the different learning preferences.

So why bother? Do different learning styles have an impact on a student's experience in school? In short, yes. Different learning styles have a significant impact on a student's experience in school because once a student understands his/her preferred method of information input and output, he/she can more effectively and more efficiently approach his/her studies with greater opportunities for success. However, if a student never knows his/her learning style, he/she can find him/herself using ineffective strategies and techniques—or worse yet, using no strategies or techniques at all—that can lead to failed attempts at success.

For instance, if a student is aware of his/her visual preference for learning, then he/she knows listening to an educator's lectures is insufficient in the quest to transfer knowledge. First, visual and read/write preferences tend to complement each other (just as do auditory and kinesthetic preferences). As such, it is common for someone to have a visual preference as well as a read/write preference or for someone to have an auditory preference in addition to a kinesthetic preference.

Therefore, for example, once a student knows he/she has a visual preference, he/she knows he/she needs to not only pay attention to a lecture but also have available during the lecture reference materials such as the textbook or any readings that support the lecture. This student also knows it's imperative that he/she take notes during the lecture because unlike the student with an auditory preference, one with a writing or read/write preference can listen with rapt attention to the lecturer but unless he/she takes notes, he/she can walk out of class and recall very little to virtually none of the lecture's content.

A student's experience and success in school is greatly impacted by not only whether a student knows his/her learning style but also if he/she knows how to take that information to drive how to perform inside and outside of the classroom in a manner that's consistent with how he/she prefers to learn.

BONUS MESSAGE: What does this mean for professionals who are listening to your presentations? It means they will want you to present the information in a variety of ways. Have opportunities for them to read material, opportunities for them to talk either to you or with each other, opportunities for them to write, and opportunities for them to manipulate objects or to stand and/or move.

Still not convinced? Don't think your students would be convinced? Here's the one thing you should tell incoming college students about learning styles and thriving in their own way of learning. The single most important step you can take to set-up yourself for success—regardless of whether you attend a technical school, a community college, an online school, a four-year university, or any other institution—is to find out how you learn best. Period. When you know your learning style, you know how to take control of your education and your future. You know what works for you and what does not. You know what to do in class and how to do it. You know how to study. You know where to focus your efforts You no longer wonder what's the most effective way to spend your time after class. You no longer get frustrated about how you should prepare for an exam. You no longer need others to tell you the actions you should take to be an accomplished student. In short, you are fully empowered and have a personal plan for academic success.

When this happens, it frees the educator up to focus more on what you do best and that is to facilitate learning in your chosen discipline with full vigor, gusto, and power!

DAY 30 SIZZLERS

1. Should your presentations include only you speaking? Should it also include a slide deck, conversations from the audience as well as opportunities for the audience to write and move? Why or why not?

   _____

   _____

   _____

2. How will your audience respond if you attend to all preferences in the room and include opportunities for the audience members to engage with each other?

   _____

   _____

   _____

3. What are meaningful questions you can ask your audiences, based on the content you present, that will get them talking or writing down ideas?

   _____

   _____

   _____

4. How will you feel differently about your presentations if you adhere to the rule that you do not have to be the one who does all the talking in a presentation?

_____

_____

_____

5. What will you do differently in your next presentation that you did not do in your last one?

_____

_____

_____

DAY 31
Professional Women, Here's How Confidence Looks
effective communication | personal branding

Confidence is a strength and a certainty one has about herself that is present regardless of her title, stature, background, or past or present circumstances. Confidence is an air about a person that makes everyone want to be around her because she is not haughty, she is not arrogant, and she may not be the thinnest or the most beautiful in the room; but because she is the one who knows her worth, who knows the worth of others and uplifts them, and she knows everything about her and that for which she stands matters, her confidence is undeniable.

Professional women can build their confidence by consistently, looking and sounding unstoppable. This means adopting the practice of always having your shoulders back, your head up, and your eyes laser-focused, especially when you speak. Every single time—no matter where you are and no matter to whom you speak.

Eliminate the "uh's" and "um's" otherwise known as filler words; because they make you sound and feel less confident.

Make statements that sound firm, not flimsy, which means intentionally using power words in your language. For example, say, "I know," or "I trust," not "I think" or "I hope."

Avoid talking through your noise and unnecessarily using a high-pitched voice; use a more measured, in-control, lower octave.

Eliminate uptalk or high-rising terminals so every sentence you say does not sound like a question but sounds like a definitive statement dripping with authority and conviction.

Even when you do not feel on top of the world, never give that impression.

Always ask yourself "How do I want to feel, and for what do I want to be remembered?"

The options are common and unexceptional or confident and unshakable. You choose.

DAY 31 SIZZLERS

1. What can you do today to build your personal brand and your personal confidence?

   _____

   _____

   _____

2. What words and/or phrases you need to eliminate from your vocabulary to, when eliminated, make you sound more confident and in control?

   _____

   _____

   _____

3. What should you do differently with the sound of your voice to sound more confident?

   _____

   _____

   _____

4. What must you do, even if you do not feel your absolute best, in order to project confidence to others?

   _____

   _____

   _____

5. When people interact with you, how do you want them to feel? For what do you want to be remembered?

_____

_____

_____

ABOUT THE AUTHOR

Bridgett McGowen is an award-winning international professional speaker; a 2019 Forbes Coaches Council official member; and the founder and owner of BMcTALKS Academy where she helps professional women be the most engaging, dynamic, incredible communicators ever!

Bridgett has been a professional speaker since 2001 and has spoken on programs alongside prominent figures such as former President Barack Obama, Deepak Chopra, Alex Rodriguez (A-Rod), Oprah Winfrey, Shonda Rhimes, Katie Couric, and Janelle Monae.

The prestigious University of Texas at Austin presented her with a Master Presenter Award; Canada-based One Woman has presented her with two Fearless Woman Awards; and she has facilitated hundreds of workshops, keynote and commencement addresses, conference sessions, trainings, and webinars to thousands of students and professionals who are positioned all around the globe.

Bridgett's expertise and presentations have been sought after by companies, post-secondary institutions, and organizations such as Vanguard Investments, LifeLock, Symantec, Kentucky Fried Chicken, McGraw-Hill Education, LinkedIn Local, Association for Talent Development, Doña

Ana Community College, National Association of Women Sales Professionals, Independence University, Turnitin, National Association of Black Accountants, and Society for Human Resource Management (SHRM). She has been quoted by Transizion, has contributed to UpJourney, and has appeared as a guest on The Training and Learning Development Company's TLDCast as well as Phoenix Business Radio to showcase her expertise in the professional speaking industry. Her work in professional speaking and public speaking coaching has been highlighted by VoyagePhoenix Magazine; award-winning branding and consulting agency, Catalyst; The Startup Growth; and her alma mater, Prairie View A&M University, the second oldest institution of higher education in the state of Texas.

Bridgett has also taught for the Texas A&M University System, Lone Star College System, and University of Phoenix. She has earned a bachelor's degree in Communication and a master's degree; is a Forbes contributor; is a member of Alpha Kappa Alpha Sorority, Incorporated; and is the president of her local Toastmasters club.

Bridgett is also the author of *REAL TALK: What Other Experts Won't Tell You About How to Make Presentations That Sizzle*, which sold out within minutes of her presentation concluding at the 76th Annual Association for Talent Development's International Conference and Exposition in Washington, D.C.

Bridgett's mission now is to help as many professional women as possible get the tools and skills they need to master their messages so that they can turn their voices into powerhouses, inspire millions, and build serious skill sets and mindsets that will lead to more and more opportunities.

Bridgett lives with her family in the Phoenix, Arizona area, and she absolutely loves beautiful sunsets.

WANT MORE?

Thank you for purchasing your copy of *Rise and Sizzle: Daily Communication and Presentation Strategies for Sales, Business, and Higher Ed Pros.*

If you are looking to further improve your speaking and presentation skills with expert guidance, then check out …

- ***REAL TALK: What Other Experts Won't Tell You About How to Make Presentations That Sizzle*** also written by Bridgett McGowen. Visit www.bmctalks.com to purchase your copy today!

- **Master Your Message**, a fully-online, self-paced program produced by BMcTALKS Academy. Visit bmctalks-academy.teachable.com to learn about Master Your message and all BMcTALKS Academy online course offerings.

You've got this!

Made in the USA
Columbia, SC
30 January 2020